John the Baptizer

BIBLE STUDY GUIDE

From the Bible-teaching ministry of

Charles R. Swindoll

INSIGHT FOR LIVING

Charles R. Swindoll is a graduate of Dallas Theological Seminary and has served in pastorates in Texas, Massachusetts, and California since 1963. He has served as senior pastor of the First Evangelical Free Church of Fullerton, California, since 1971. Chuck's radio program, "Insight for Living," began in 1979. In addition to his church and radio ministries, Chuck enjoys writing. He has authored numerous books and booklets on a variety of subjects.

Based on the outlines and transcripts of Chuck's sermons, the study guide text is co-authored by Bryce Klabunde, a graduate of Biola University and Dallas Theological Seminary. He also wrote the Living Insights sections.

Editor in Chief:
Cynthia Swindoll

Director, Communications Division:
Deedee Synder

Coauthor of Text:
Bryce Klabunde

Project Manager:
Alene Cooper

Assistant Editor:
Wendy Peterson

Project Coordinator:
Susan Nelson

Senior Copy Editor:
Glenda Schlahta

Assistant Print Production Manager:
John Norton

Copy Editor:
Brown Suffield

Printer:
Frye and Smith

Designer:
Ken Perry

Production Artists:
Cindy Ford and Robert McGuire

Typographer:
Bob Haskins

Unless otherwise identified, all Scripture references are from the New American Standard Bible, © The Lockman Foundation 1960, 1962, 1963, 1968, 1971, 1972, 1973, 1975, 1977. Used by permission.

An effort has been made to locate sources and obtain permission where necessary for the quotations used in this book. In the event of any unintentional omission, a modification will gladly be incorporated in future printings.

ISBN 0-8499-8425-4

Printed in the United States of America.

COVER PAINTING: *Preaching of St. John the Baptist* by Allesandro Allori.

CONTENTS

INTRODUCTION

Bible characters continue to be one of my favorite studies. It is possible that you feel the same. There's nothing quite like seeing how God prepares, trains, uses, and rewards His chosen instruments. And how relevent they often are! Frequently, we feel as though the very things they went through are like pages out of our own diaries.

The Baptizer is like none other, however. He stands alone . . . sometimes, aloof. His amazing conception in Elizabeth's womb, his early years in the lonely, rugged wilderness, mixed with his unique appearance and style, must have caused tongues to wag all across the countryside. As the forerunner of Messiah, John had the unenviable task of preparing the way of the Lord. But God knew the kind of man to choose and He trained him well. When John spoke, people sat up and took notice.

I hope you come to appreciate the man as much as I have. May each study help you get better acquainted. And most of all, may your admiration for Christ take on new dimensions as you realize the role His forerunner was called to fill. Pay close attention to the balance between humility and courage in this prophet. Both are rare traits in our day of ego trips and compromise.

Chuck Swindoll

PUTTING TRUTH INTO ACTION

Knowledge apart from application falls short of God's desire for His children. He wants us to apply what we learn so that we will change and grow. This study guide was prepared with these goals in mind. As you go through the following pages, we hope your desire to discover biblical truth will grow as your understanding of God's Word increases, and that you will be encouraged to apply what you've learned.

To assist you in your study, we've included a section called **Living Insights** at the end of each lesson. These exercises will challenge you to study further and to think of specific ways to put your discoveries into action.

On occasion a lesson is followed by a **Digging Deeper** section, which gives you additional information and resources to probe further into some issues raised in that lesson.

There are many ways to use this guide—in personal devotions, group studies, discussions with friends and family, and Sunday school classes. And, of course, it's an ideal study aid when you're listening to its corresponding "Insight for Living" radio series.

To benefit most from this study guide, we would encourage you to consider it a spiritual journal. That's why we've included space in the **Living Insights** for recording your thoughts and discoveries. We hope you'll return to those sections often for review and encouragement as you continue to grow in your walk with Christ.

Bryce Klabunde

Bryce Klabunde
Coauthor of Text
Author of Living Insights

John the Baptizer

Chapter 1

A MOST UNUSUAL BABY

Luke 1:5–25, 57–64, 76–80

If there is one name the whole world associates with greatness, it is that of Alfred Nobel. Yet few remember him for his own achievement, the invention of dynamite; instead, he is famous for recognizing the greatness of others. Each year on the anniversary of his death, prizes are awarded by a provision in his will for outstanding accomplishments in the fields of physics, medicine, chemistry, literature, and peace. Through his philanthropy we have come to know names like Pierre and Marie Curie, Albert Einstein, Rudyard Kipling, Ernest Hemingway, and Mother Teresa.

Jesus also gave His version of the Nobel Prize. But the laureate who received this honor was no scholar or scientist. Austere and terrifying, he roamed the Judean wastelands as a hermit and was considered an outcast by his people. Even so, he was "sent from God" (John 1:6), and upon his head Jesus placed the crown of greatness when He declared:

> "Truly, I say to you, among those born of women there has not arisen anyone greater than John the Baptist." (Matt. 11:11a)

What made John the Baptizer[1] great? As a minister, he had none of the symbols we associate with success—no books, no evangelistic crusades, no congenial sermons. Instead, his message was simple and often redundant. Moreover, he was unattractive, unkempt, and . . . well, unusual.

But as we spade into his life, we will uncover golden characteristics of greatness: humility, integrity, purity, diligence, simplicity, vulnerability, and vision. He was a true prophet from God; and his message, though brief, lingers still.

---

1. In this study we will refer to John as the "Baptizer" rather than the "Baptist," which more clearly specifies his task as one who baptizes.

1

Profile of a Prophet

Today, self-proclaimed prophets come and go with each toss of the morning news. Most of us do not take them seriously; but when a true prophet like John appears, he cannot be overlooked. How can we recognize a true prophet? Scripture gives three characterizing qualifications.

Prophets in General

First: *Genuine prophets were selected by God and personally called to the task.* The prophet Jeremiah wrote concerning his own calling,

> Now the word of the Lord came to me saying,
> "Before I formed you in the womb I knew you,
> And before you were born I consecrated you;
> I have appointed you a prophet to the nations."
> (Jer. 1:4–5)

God's divine selection had nothing to do with social standing, inheritance, or talent. Some prophets were even reluctant to accept God's call—Jonah, for example. Others, like Amos, who was a herdsman and fig-picker from Tekoa, were definitely not "preacher material," yet the calling of God was unmistakably on their lives (see Amos 7:14–15).

Second: *True prophets spoke for God as His personal mouthpiece.* A clear example of this is in God's promise to Moses.

> " 'I will raise up a prophet from among their country-
> men like you, and I will put My words in his mouth,
> and he shall speak to them all that I command him.' "
> (Deut. 18:18)

Whether they even understood the words they said, one thing was sure—true prophets were speaking God's words. If they made a mistake in their prophecy, their words were not God's and they were not true prophets. They were labeled false prophets and were not only to be ignored, but terminated (see Deut. 18:19–22).

Third: *They operated as loners and not in groups.* Prophets were the conscience of their society; but when the people ignored their consciences, prophets found themselves ignored as well. True prophets were trailblazers; they were God's select soldiers—courageous, undaunted, yet alone.

> Prophets had to be people of outstanding character,
> great minds, and courageous souls. They had to be

this by nature and then, being dedicated to God, they became still greater because of the tasks and special provisions assigned them. Thus they became the towering giants of Israel, the formers of public opinion, the leaders through days of darkness, people distinguished from all those about them either in Israel or other nations of the day.[2]

John in Particular

John met these qualifications of a true prophet. He received his call directly from God (John 1:6), he was God's mouthpiece (vv. 7–8), and he stood as a lone voice delivering the message God had given him (v. 15). This message had been predicted by Isaiah seven centuries earlier.

> A voice is calling,
> "Clear the way for the Lord in the wilderness;
> Make smooth in the desert a highway for our God.
> Let every valley be lifted up,
> And every mountain and hill be made low;
> And let the rough ground become a plain,
> And the rugged terrain a broad valley;
> Then the glory of the Lord will be revealed,
> And all flesh will see it together;
> For the mouth of the Lord has spoken."
> (Isa. 40:3–5)

According to this passage, John had three responsibilities: to clear the way for the Lord, to prepare the way for the Lord, and to get out of the way of the Lord![3] This divine task was urgent, for the religious leaders had mounded huge obstacles of legalism that hindered faith, and the people's immorality made them unprepared for the Messiah's arrival.

Like the people in John's day, we have mountains of pride and valleys of unbelief that need to be leveled too. John the Baptizer can be our human bulldozer—crushing obstinate hypocrisy, blasting through superficial rhetoric, and filling in pits of despair. If we are

2. Leon J. Wood, *The Prophets of Israel* (Grand Rapids, Mich.: Baker Book House, 1979), p. 16.

3. George Goodman, as cited by J. Oswald Sanders in *Robust in Faith* (Chicago, Ill.: Moody Press, 1965), pp. 175–76.

willing, God's Spirit can use this man to smooth our pride, shape our will, and prepare our hearts to meet Jesus face-to-face.

Birth of a Baby

It certainly follows that such an extraordinary man would have an extraordinary beginning. John's birth was a twinkle of light in a world engulfed in moral darkness. Let's step back and take a look at life in John's day.

His Nation and Times

Throughout the history of Israel, God had spoken to His people through prophets. However, at the time of John's birth, about four hundred years had passed since God's last message had been heard through the prophet Malachi.

With no fresh word from the Lord, religion in John's day had gone stale. The Mosaic Law seemed dusty and irrelevant, so religious leaders "helped God out" by telling the people how the Scriptures should be interpreted. Over time, these interpretations became as revered as Holy Scripture. However, they were like saltwater to someone dying of thirst. Man's traditions had contaminated God's truth, leaving the people with a bad taste in their mouths and a spiritual thirst in their hearts.

Politically, the people were hapless victims of power-hungry tyrants. John's birth came toward the end of the reign of Herod the Great, who was as well-known for his towering buildings as his limitless vile. It was a time of ruthless backstabbing and moral depravity. But, it was also a time for God's glory to shine through a faithful priest and his barren wife.

His Father and Mother

While Herod was sadistically murdering his own sons in Jerusalem, just outside of town an aging priest and his wife lamented their infertility. Concerning this couple, Zacharias and Elizabeth, the Bible says,

> And they were both righteous in the sight of God,
> walking blamelessly in all the commandments and
> requirements of the Lord. (Luke 1:6)

And yet this godly pair had no children. Every barren woman can understand Elizabeth's silent sorrow as time erased her hopes of pregnancy.

Then . . .

An angel. A message. A pregnant wife. A speechless husband.

Zacharias had entered the temple to pray and make the incense offering,[4] and while he was performing this sacred duty, the angel Gabriel suddenly appeared to him and said,

> "Do not be afraid, Zacharias, for your petition has been heard, and your wife Elizabeth will bear you a son, and you will give him the name John. And you will have joy and gladness, and many will rejoice at his birth. For he will be great in the sight of the Lord, and he will drink no wine or liquor; and he will be filled with the Holy Spirit, while yet in his mother's womb." (vv. 13b–15)

God answered not only Zacharias' priestly prayer for the redemption of Israel, but also his longing for a son. All of this was too wonderful for Zacharias to believe (v. 18). So because of his unbelief, God caused him to remain mute until John's birth (v. 20).

His Calling and Role

Gabriel's words to Zacharias also revealed the baby's extraordinary calling.

> "And he will turn back many of the sons of Israel to the Lord their God. And it is he who will go as a forerunner before Him in the spirit and power of Elijah, to turn the hearts of the fathers back to the children,[5] and the disobedient to the attitude of the righteous; so as to make ready a people prepared for the Lord." (vv. 16–17)

John's mission grew out of the prophecies of the Hebrew Scriptures. For thousands of years, men of God had blown the trumpet

---

4. "The incense offering took place twice daily, early morning and mid-afternoon (Exod. 30:7f). To be the offering priest was an honour which some priests never received and none were permitted more than once. As the sacrificed animal burned outside, the offering priest poured incense over a live coal on the altar within the Holy Place. As the smoke arose, he prayed some set prayer for the blessing, peace, and messianic redemption of Israel." E. Earle Ellis, *The Gospel of Luke*, rev. ed., New Century Bible Commentary series (1974; reprint, Grand Rapids, Mich.: William B. Eerdmans Publishing Co., 1983), p. 68. See also Norval Geldenhuys, *Commentary on the Gospel of Luke* (1951; reprint, Grand Rapids, Mich.: William B. Eerdmans Publishing Co., 1972), pp. 62–64.

5. This is a direct reference to the words of Malachi four hundred years earlier (see Mal. 4:6).

call, "God will come; God will come." That same dusty, tarnished trumpet was now handed to John, who would sound the new message, "God is here."

His Birth and Growth

For nine long months Zacharias said not one word. Then eight days after the birth of his son, at the circumcision ceremony, he wrote "John" on a tablet instead of the expected "Zacharias" for the boy's name, and immediately he began to speak.[6] Zacharias proved his faith in the angel's prophecy concerning his son; by naming him John, he relinquished his prerogative to determine the boy's future. John belonged to God.

Unlike any other person—apart from Jesus—John was filled with the Spirit from conception to birth. And as he grew, the Spirit drew him to the wilderness, where he stayed until his thirties.[7] John's life in the desert seems eccentric to us, but in his world, his camel-hair clothes with the leather belt and his locust-and-honey diet were recognized as characteristics of a holy man.[8]

In the lonely wasteland of the snakes and jackals, John's greatness emerged. Through his willingness to be used by God, he became the conscience of an entire nation. All eyes were focused on this desert evangelist as he humbly proclaimed the coming of the King of Kings and Lord of Lords.

Lessons from a Life

Unlike John, no angels appeared to announce our birth, nor were there prophecies concerning our life's occupation. All the same, we can learn several lessons about greatness from John's story.

First: *It is in the worst of times that God's best servants emerge.* John's prophetic ministry required a man of unfeigned character, a

---

6. When God loosed Zacharias' tongue, months of pent-up zeal poured out in praise to the Lord (see vv. 67–79).

7. Because Luke 3:23 says Jesus was "about thirty years of age" when He began His ministry, and because Mary and Elizabeth were pregnant together (Luke 1:24–31), we can conclude that John was also about thirty at this time. See Alexander Whyte, *Bible Characters from the New Testament* (New Canaan, Conn.: Keats Publishing, 1981), p. 27.

8. John came in the "spirit and power of Elijah" (Luke 1:17), which was evidenced not only by his ministry but also by his lifestyle (see 2 Kings 1:8). "His food consisted of locusts (cf. Lev. 11:21–22, where they are listed among clean foods) and wild honey. The wild honey is bees' honey and not, as has sometimes been suggested, carob pods or sap from various trees in the area." Walter W. Wessel, "Mark," in *The Expositor's Bible Commentary* (Grand Rapids, Mich.: Zondervan Publishing House, Regency Reference Library, 1984), vol. 8, p. 620.

man who was aware of his times and yet unpolluted by them. The times in which we live are equal to John's in hypocrisy, moral depravity, injustice, and corruption. These days require men and women equal to John in character and moral fiber who will join the fight on the front line.

Second: *There is no better training for depth of character than obscurity, loneliness, and solitude.* God's boot camp is in the wilderness. Strong character is wrestled out in the lonely places where no one sees and no one hears. John's shining moment came when he baptized Jesus, but endless days of obscurity prepared him for that privilege. Similarly, we shouldn't neglect times of silence and enrichment, for they are the foundation of honor.

Third: *The rarest yet greatest quality of Christ's representative is a willingness to be eclipsed.* Just as the sun's brightness eclipses the glow of the morning star, so should Christ's glory outshine our own. To clear the way and prepare the way as John did is difficult, but the real challenge is to get out of the way. Let humility grow as the light of Jesus spreads through you to everyone near, and let the Lord build in you the qualities of greatness.

 ## Living Insights STUDY ONE

What would happen if John the Baptizer was the guest speaker at your church next Sunday? Can you picture John—with his matted hair, smelly camel coat, and filthy feet—munching on a handful of locusts while greeting folks between services? Who would want to shake his hand, much less invite him for Sunday lunch!

But John's appearance would not be the only thing making him seem bizarre. His convictions and self-denial would make him stand out just as much as his affinity for bugs and honey. In our world, it is almost considered weird to have high standards. Just try mentioning chastity in a group of swinging singles, or integrity to money-hungry power brokers, and see the kind of looks you get.

Years ago, however, G. K. Chesterton asserted that it is not the one with convictions who is out of touch, it is the rest of the world. "Millions of mild black coated men call themselves sane and sensible merely because they always catch the fashionable insanity, because they are hurried into madness after madness by the maelstrom of the world."[9]

9. G. K. Chesterton, in *The Quotable Chesterton*, ed. George J. Marlin, Richard P. Rabatin, and John L. Swan (San Francisco, Calif.: Ignatius Press, 1986), p. 216.

Think about the phrase "fashionable insanity." Doesn't it describe our world today? In the midst of such a world gone mad, beaming its craziness into your living room through the media, how can you hold on to your convictions and maintain your spiritual sanity? For an answer, look to Zacharias' prayer concerning his son, John, and the coming Messiah in Luke 1:76–79, and respond to the following questions.

John the Baptizer was to prepare the way for the coming of Jesus. According to verse 77, what is Jesus' mission?

_____

_____

Zacharias also says that Jesus will be the "Sunrise from on high" who comes warming the world with the "tender mercy of our God" (v. 78). What two ways will Jesus accomplish this, according to verse 79?

1. _____

2. _____

Isn't that encouraging? In the midst of this world's craziness, Jesus is our light and our guide. That's what John the Baptizer came to announce. How can we maintain our spiritual sanity? By holding on, by *clinging*, to Christ.

 Living Insights STUDY TWO

There is something purifying about the desert. Its starkness makes the sky bluer, the water more precious, the flowers richer, the evenings more refreshing. Things seem clearer, untangled. Unlike a cluttered forest, the desert is vast and free. This is where John the Baptizer met God.

How often our lives resemble a complex forest with our snarled schedules and confining expectations. It is impossible to see very far in the forest; but in the desert, things far away seem so close you could touch them. Could it be that you need some time to retreat to the desert, where you can once again catch a glimpse of God's mountain, clear your head, and sense God's spirit-lifting touch?

In Mark 6:31a, Jesus said to His disciples,

> "Come away by yourselves to a lonely place and rest a while."

Why would He say this?

> For there were many people coming and going, and they did not even have time to eat. (v. 31b)

Sound like your house? Perhaps it's time for a trip to John's desert, time to retreat for your spiritual and emotional health. Now don't let this thought slip by as a nice but impractical idea. There are many ways you can "come away to a lonely place"—you just need to be creative. To help spark your creativity, use this time to put your thoughts on paper, focusing on the following questions. Where will your place of retreat be? When can you go there? What questions will you ask God? What Scripture will you meditate on?

_____

_____

_____

_____

_____

_____

_____

_____

_____

_____

_____

Experience the desert and meet God in the lonely places.

Chapter 2

PROFILE OF A STRANGE EVANGELIST

Mark 1:1–8

G ray suits with briefcases weaving through ranks of smart-looking skirts crowd the city streets in search of lunch. Hustling to beat the noon rush, two gray suits absorbed in the deal of the century inadvertently meet a disturbing stare.

"Oh no, not him again," says the Senior suit, averting his eyes.

"Who is this guy? What a nut!" says the Junior suit, a newcomer.

The two are trapped at the crosswalk. Can't go around, can't go back. They are face-to-face with the Street Preacher. Fixing his glare, the wild-eyed anomaly steps toward his subjects. As he slowly raises his stiffened arm and points a terrifying finger, his voice booms: "Guilllllty!" Then he walks away.

Red light changes to green. The Senior, relieved, strides into the intersection. Picking up where he left off, he notices the Junior still on the curb, eyes riveted on the departing judge.

"Don't let it get to you," says the experienced one.

"How did he know?" says the other, half laughing—half worried.[1]

The Beginning of a Revolution

If John the Baptizer were alive, he would be more like this urban street preacher than like the polished, silver-tongued evangelists we are accustomed to. We would probably consider him strange and intrusive, but John's style of preaching was for a unique, God-ordained purpose. He was to spearhead a spiritual revolution, which required making people ready to receive the coming Messiah. This was the mission of John, to arouse the world's slumbering conscience, causing it to yearn for a new spiritual order.

Mark describes the onset of this revolution simply, yet profoundly, as "The beginning of the gospel of Jesus Christ, the Son of God" (Mark 1:1). Then he introduces John the Baptizer as the

---

1. Adapted from Karl Menninger, in *Whatever Became of Sin?* (New York, N.Y.: Bantam Books, 1973), pp. 1–2.

forerunner of this glorious gospel. John's commission comes from the prophecies of Isaiah, which describe John as the messenger preparing the way for Jesus.

> As it is written in Isaiah the prophet,
> "Behold, I send My messenger before Your face,
> Who will prepare Your way;
> The voice of one crying in the wilderness,
> 'Make ready the way of the Lord,
> Make His paths straight.'" (Mark 1:2–3)[2]

Though the locust-and-honey-eating John is not the type of person we would envision for this position, he was God's man for the job. Remember, God's ways are not our ways (Isa. 55:8–9). His choice for the ideal candidate for a job may often leave us scratching our heads, but if we open our hearts and minds to His decisions, we can gain invaluable wisdom.

With this in mind, let's take a closer look at the man God selected to begin this revolution.

The Evangelist Who Was Responsible

John's short ministry was the climax of a life of fanatic devotion. He spent the majority of his days in the desert; his appearance became disheveled, his skin leathery, and his face weatherworn. But in his strange way, he was an arrow pointing to Jesus . . . and that's all he was created to be.

His Arrival

> John the Baptist appeared in the wilderness preaching a baptism of repentance for the forgiveness of sins. And all the country of Judea was going out to him, and all the people of Jerusalem; and they were being baptized by him in the Jordan River, confessing their sins. (Mark 1:4–5)

John appeared without fanfare, yet he soon received widespread notoriety through his unique preaching and unusual practice of baptizing in the Jordan River. In fact, the kind of baptism he was performing was normally associated with the induction of proselytes—

---

2. This prophecy is a combination of three passages: Exodus 23:20, Isaiah 40:3, and Malachi 3:1. Mark attributes the quote to Isaiah to emphasize him as the foremost prophet.

Gentiles who were converting to Judaism. John shocked the Jews by requiring them to participate in this baptism, implying that they needed the same kind of repentance as Gentiles. William Barclay highlights the significance of this for us.

> The amazing thing about John's baptism was that he, a Jew, was asking Jews to submit to that which only a Gentile was supposed to need. John had made the tremendous discovery that to be a Jew in the racial sense was not to be a member of God's chosen people; a Jew might be in exactly the same position as a Gentile; not the *Jewish* life, but the *cleansed* life belonged to God. (emphasis added)[3]

His Audience

Through John's radical message and baptism ministry, many hearts were genuinely softened and many people truly repented. Others, however, let their hearts remain hard, and to them John turned in scorn, convicting them of their hypocrisy.

> But when he saw many of the Pharisees and Sadducees coming for baptism, he said to them, "You brood of vipers, who warned you to flee from the wrath to come? Therefore bring forth fruit in keeping with repentance; and do not suppose that you can say to yourselves, 'We have Abraham for our father'; for I say to you, that God is able from these stones to raise up children to Abraham." (Matt. 3:7–9)

John's statements surely would have made the tabloids—"Baptizer Slanders Local Leaders: 'You bunch of snakes!'" But John was making an important point: being of the lineage of Abraham did not guarantee salvation. Only genuine repentance[4] and faith could do that.

Since repentance is so vital to a right relationship with God, John explained in detail what it truly is. First, to the multitudes,

---

3. William Barclay, *The Gospel of Mark*, rev. ed., The Daily Study Bible series (Philadelphia, Pa.: Westminster Press, 1975), p. 14.

4. The Greek word for *repentance, metanoia,* means "a change of mind, regret, remorse." But John's repentance goes beyond feeling sorrowful about one's sin. Like the Old Testament prophets, John called the nation to return to the Lord through obedience (compare Zech. 1:3). See C. E. B. Cranfield, *The Gospel According to Saint Mark*, rev. ed. (1959; reprint, London, England: Cambridge University Press, 1972), pp. 44–45.

he said that true repentance is seen in benevolent deeds toward others.

> And the multitudes were questioning him, saying, "Then what shall we do?" And he would answer and say to them, "Let the man who has two tunics share with him who has none; and let him who has food do likewise." (Luke 3:10–11)

Second, to a group of tax-collectors—whose corruption was legend in those days—he said that true repentance is seen in honesty.

> "Collect no more than what you have been ordered to." (v. 13)

And third, to some soldiers—who were known for taking whatever they wanted—he said that true repentance is seen in honor and contentment.

> "Do not take money from anyone by force, or accuse anyone falsely, and be content with your wages." (v. 14b)

John's message of repentance is specific and practical. It involves more than taking a dip in the Jordan and having a spiritual experience. It means changing one's life. In all the categories of life—as a spouse, parent, roommate, employee, or boss—we are to practice our Christian beliefs, not just give verbal assent to them. If repentance is true, then it will impact our giving, our attitudes, and our treatment of others. It may begin with a sorrowful heart, but it must end with determined action.

His Appearance

John not only spoke like a prophet of God, he looked the part. His rugged, austere message matched his rugged, austere life. Unlike the pampered orators of his day, and some religious leaders of our day, John was willing to abide by the same principles he preached.

This integrity, however, is important for more than just religious leaders. Although we are not all called to walk around in camel-hair tunics and eat insects, we are called to be "Jesus" to whomever we meet, and that means we should model what we believe.[5]

---

5. Compare 1 John 1:6—"If we say that we have fellowship with Him and yet walk in the darkness, we lie and do not practice the truth."

His Announcement

As well as calling people to true repentance, John's mission was to announce the arrival of the Messiah. First, John proclaimed, *He is mightier than I.*

> And he was preaching, and saying, "After me One is coming who is mightier than I." (Mark 1:7a)

Hardened by the endless buffeting of the wilderness, John had considerable physical strength. Yet the coming Christ would surpass John's natural power, demonstrating a supernaturally charged inner strength.

John next said of the coming Christ, *He is greater than I.*

> "And I am not fit to stoop down and untie the thong of His sandals." (v. 7b)

Only a slave knelt to undo his master's shoes; yet, in light of the greatness of Christ, John felt he was unworthy even of that humiliating duty.[6]

Then John said, *He is holier than I.*

> "I baptized you with water; but He will baptize you with the Holy Spirit." (v. 8)

John washed the people with water, but Christ would transform them on the inside, making their innermost beings flow with rivers of living water.

Some Similarities Today

Underneath the surface, our world isn't so different from that of John's. In fact, three similarities stand out with striking clarity.

First: *In the hall of faith, mavericks still abound.* John was a maverick, not so much because he acted like a nut, but because he dared to live out his convictions. In a day of moral compromise and stifling mediocrity, we also need men and women who go against the grain—who stand for what they believe.

Second: *In the ranks of the faithful, hypocrites still appear.* The Pharisees and Sadducees hung around John's ministry just like their

---

6. Jewish law sheds additional light on John's statement: "'All services which a slave does for his master a pupil should do for his teacher, with the exception of undoing his shoes.'" Rabbi Joshua B. Levi, as quoted by Cranfield in *The Gospel According to Saint Mark*, p. 48.

contemporary counterparts hang around churches today. We must recognize that Christ's body is going to be full of hypocrites; that is why the authentic person is so in demand.

Third: *In the lives of the fruitful, humility is still appropriate.* As a result of his extraordinary ministry, John experienced an avalanche of popularity. He could have started believing that he was the Messiah, yet he understood his humble position and, instead, kept pointing to Jesus. Notoriety may come our way too, so we must be wary of the temptation to admire ourselves to the exclusion of others and Christ. The proud person wants to always point in the mirror; Christ needs servants who will point to Him instead. Let's remember to give credit to others and to present Christ as the One who is mightier, greater, and holier than we could ever be.

 Living Insights   STUDY ONE

In a poll taken on spiritual life in America, George Gallup uncovered some startling results. A majority of Americans believe Christ rose from the dead and is a living Presence today, yet very few translate that belief into action. Gallup remarks,

> There's little difference in ethical behavior be-
> tween the churched and the unchurched. There's as
> much pilferage and dishonesty among the churched
> as the unchurched. And I'm afraid that applies pretty
> much across the board: religion, per se, is not really
> life changing. People cite it as important, for in-
> stance, in overcoming depression—but it doesn't
> have primacy in determining behavior.[7]

How does it make you feel to read, "Religion, per se, is not really life changing?" Are there areas of your life religion has been unable to change? If so, what are they?

_____

_____

_____

_____

7. George H. Gallup, "Vital Signs," *Leadership*, Fall 1987, p. 17.

In his book *I Surrender*, Patrick Morley writes that the church's integrity problem is in the misconception "that we can add Christ to our lives, but not subtract sin. It is a change in belief without a change in behavior." He goes on to say, "It is revival without reformation, without repentance."[8]

The apostle Paul had a religious experience on the road to Damascus, in which he encountered the living Christ in a spectacular way. In that experience he "added" Christ to his life. But he did not stop there; his initial faith produced action. Read his recollection of the incident in Acts 26:12–20, and especially notice verse 20. From this last verse, what are the three points Paul was declaring in his message?

1. _____

2. _____

3. _____

Notice any similarity to John the Baptizer's sermon? It is the same message: we must repent, turn to God, and then obey. Reflect on the areas of your life you wrote down earlier. Commit them to Christ, and surrender them to Him so that you can start changing today.

 ## Living Insights
STUDY TWO

Archimedes, the Greek mathematician who invented the lever and pulley, confidently stated, "Give me a place on which to stand, and I will move the earth."[9] Can that be true? Can one man with the aid of giant levers and pulleys actually shift the weight of the earth? Theoretically, yes. But practically, no.

Often our Christianity seems to be just as theoretical. The sinful habits in our lives burden us, and, unable to carry the weight of them, we are crushed instead. Theoretically, we are supposed to be able to move mountains; but practically, the mountains don't budge.

8. Patrick M. Morley, *I Surrender: Submitting to Christ in the Details of Life* (Brentwood, Tenn.: Wolgemuth and Hyatt, Publishers, 1990), p. 14.

9. Archimedes, *The Little, Brown Book of Anecdotes*, ed. Clifton Fadiman (Boston, Mass.: Little, Brown and Co., 1985), p. 19.

However, even Archimedes will tell you that the power is not in our effort; the power is in the machine and in where we stand.

Read Luke 3:16. Compare and contrast John the Baptizer and the coming Christ. Who has the power? What is the power?

_____

_____

_____

_____

Baptism in water has no power, church programs have no power, positive thinking has no power, self-effort has no power. The "pulley and lever" of the Christian life is the Holy Spirit, and the "place on which to stand" is Christ. Therein is the power and the platform.

True repentance allows that power to work in our lives. As we admit our need, we transfer the weight of sin to Christ. Then, as we focus on obeying Christ, His Spirit will take care of moving the mountains of sin in our lives.

In what specific areas do you need to obey Christ this week?

_____

_____

_____

Archimedes' secret was to concentrate on the machine, not the weight. Let's make our own Archimedean claim: "Give me Christ on whom I stand, and I can change my world!"

 ## Digging Deeper

The life of John the Baptizer becomes richer and more significant when we see him reflected in the ancient prophecies. From these passages, we can find out why the Jews so enthusiastically ran out to hear him, why he said he wasn't Elijah although Jesus said he was, why he preached in the wilderness, and why he scorned the Pharisees and Sadducees.

John the Baptizer's Popularity

The people flocked to see John because they saw in him similarities to Elijah, the ancient prophet. Based on Malachi 4:5–6, Jewish tradition taught that Elijah would literally return before the Messiah would judge the wicked and establish His everlasting kingdom. The Jews eagerly anticipated this release from oppression and entrance into a period of blessing, so they excitedly went out to see this man who was so like Elijah. From the references below, notice the parallels between John the Baptizer and Elijah.

Elijah	John
2 Kings 1:8	Matthew 3:4
Malachi 4:5	Matthew 3:7
Malachi 4:6	Luke 1:17

John the Baptizer's Identity

Despite the similarities, John said that he was not Elijah (John 1:21). But from his birth announcement, we know that John came in the "spirit and power of Elijah" (Luke 1:17). Also, Jesus said that he fulfilled the prophecies concerning the "Elijah" forerunner of Malachi 4:5 (see Matt. 11:14; 17:10–12). So who is John? Is he Elijah or not? The answer is that he is not the Elijah the Jews expected— Elijah returning from heaven—but he is the Elijah-like prophet whom Malachi predicted and Jesus validated.[10] Notice in the following verses how John fulfills the ministry of the Elijah-like prophet.

Elijah-like Prophet	John
Isaiah 40:3	John 1:23
Malachi 3:1	Matthew 11:10

John the Baptizer's Parish

John preached from the desert because it was historically a place of penance and judgment for the Jews. It signified their need to be purified so that they would be ready for the coming Messiah. Commentator William Lane underscores the meaning for us.

> As the people heed John's call and go out to him in the desert far more is involved than contrition and

---

10. J. Dwight Pentecost, *Things to Come: A Study in Biblical Eschatology* (Grand Rapids, Mich.: Zondervan Publishing House, 1958), pp. 309–13.

confession. They return to a place of judgment, the wilderness, where the status of Israel as God's beloved son must be re-established in the exchange of pride for humility. The willingness to return to the wilderness signifies the acknowledgment of Israel's history as one of disobedience and rebellion, and a desire to begin once more.[11]

John the Baptizer's Scorn of the Pharisees and Sadducees

Because baptism testified not only to repentance but also to membership in God's future kingdom, the religious leaders came to be baptized too. John, however, seeing through their pious facade, would not allow it. Their actions betrayed a lack of true repentance; so John told them that they would not enter into God's kingdom but into God's wrath (Matt. 3:7). John's message of God's wrath, as well as his message concerning God's kingdom, also relates to Old Testament predictions.

Old Testament Predictions	John
Malachi 4:1	Matthew 3:12
Malachi 4:1	Matthew 3:10
Isaiah 1:16	Matthew 3:6
Malachi 4:2	Luke 1:78
Micah 4:6–8	Matthew 3:1–2

From this overview we have seen the Baptizer from the perspective of the Old Testament. John was a bridge, joining the Old and New Testaments, spanning law and grace. And in his message we discover the timeless principles of God's relentless justice and hope-inspiring mercy.

11. William L. Lane, *The Gospel According to Mark* (Grand Rapids, Mich.: William B. Eerdmans Publishing Co., 1974), pp. 50–51.

Chapter 3

WHAT ARE THE SECRETS OF HUMILITY?

John 1:6–37; 3:22–30

In his book *The Friendship Factor*, Alan Loy McGinnis tells this poignantly revealing story about opera star Marian Anderson.

The concert impresario, Sol Hurok, liked to say that Marian Anderson hadn't simply grown great, she'd grown great simply. He says:

> A few years ago a reporter interviewed Marian and asked her to name the greatest moment in her life. I was in her dressing room at the time and was curious to hear the answer. I knew she had many big moments to choose from. There was the night Toscanini told her that hers was the finest voice of the century. There was the private concert she gave at the White House for the Roosevelts and the King and Queen of England. She had received the $10,000 Bok Award as the person who had done the most for her home town, Philadelphia. To top it all, there was that Easter Sunday in Washington when she stood beneath the Lincoln statue and sang for a crowd of 75,000, which included Cabinet members, Supreme Court Justices, and most members of Congress.

Which of those big moments did she choose?
"None of them," said Hurok. "Miss Anderson told the reporter that the greatest moment of her life was the day she went home and told her mother she wouldn't have to take in washing anymore."[1]

---

1. As quoted by Alan Loy McGinnis in *The Friendship Factor* (Minneapolis, Minn.: Augsburg Publishing House, 1979), p. 30.

What makes a person so great remain so humble? Why do so many who gain greatness lose the precious quality of humility along the way? And what are the secrets of this rare and elusive trait?

To discover the secrets of humility, we need to find and follow someone who possessed this gift, someone who attained greatness but never let go of a humble spirit. Such a person can be found in John the Baptizer; because, though he was a great man, humility sparkled in him like a precious jewel and adorned his demeanor with appealing beauty. So let's take the Baptizer as our guide and follow him through four challenging phases in his life. We'll begin our journey in the first chapter of the gospel of John.

The Man and His Mission

After five brief but profound verses about Jesus' deity, personality, and position, a sudden change in the gospel record occurs at verse 6. Here the spotlight swings over to the Baptizer, and for three short verses he takes center stage.

> There came a man, sent from God, whose name was John. He came for a witness, that he might bear witness of the light, that all might believe through him. He was not the light, but came that he might bear witness of the light. (John 1:6–8)

"There came a man." Not a superman, not even a supernatural man. Just a man. Our human tendency is to pedestalize those who are used greatly, especially someone sent from God. But John never allowed that to happen; he understood the dangers both to those who put leaders on pedestals and to those who try to stand on so shaky a foundation. John knew exactly who he was—a common, garden-variety, ordinary human being . . . just a man.[2]

His mission, however, was as extraordinary as he was ordinary. As we saw in verse 7, John's calling was to be a witness, "that he might bear witness of the light." In other words, God subpoenaed John to take the witness stand and tell the truth, the whole truth, and nothing but the truth concerning Christ—and this he did with faithfulness and integrity (see 10:41). The purpose behind his mission of truth was "that all might believe through him" (1:7b). This

2. In all the New Testament, there is not one mention of John the Baptizer performing a miracle.

was no simple and painless task; John's unflinching honesty ultimately brought him martyrdom in the dungeons of Herod Antipas.[3]

So we have an ordinary man and an extraordinary vocation . . . two uneven elements that can easily topple humility's delicate balance. Verse 8, however, restores that balance by revealing John's limitation: "He was not the light, but came that he might bear witness of the light."

All of this introduces us to the first secret of humility: *Truly humble people have a clear understanding of their mission and an acceptance of their limitations.* This doesn't mean that we're supposed to put ourselves down or grovel. It *does* mean we should be clear-minded regarding who we are, what we're to do, and what our limits are. And John illustrates this beautifully, because he knew

- He was a man, not the Messiah.

- He was John, not Jesus.

- He was a voice, not the Word.

- He was a lamp, not the Light.

Humility can sparkle in our lives, too, when we have a clear understanding of our purpose and when we fully accept our limitations.

The Role and Its Temptations

In another phase of John's life, we find him dealing with a period of high visibility in which he was called upon to fill three roles. Let's look at these roles and their humility-robbing temptations.

As a Spokesperson

The first role was that of being a spokesperson for God. When John talked, people listened. When he said something, it was worth hearing. In this role, he could have highlighted his own importance, his own sacrifices, his own accomplishments. But John 1:15 reveals a different story.

> John bore witness of Him, and cried out, saying,
> "This was He of whom I said, 'He who comes after me
> has a higher rank than I, for He existed before me.'"

---

3. A beautiful postscript to John's death is that his dream became reality; as a result of his true witness, many believed in Jesus and were saved (see John 10:41–42).

22

Just as a blind man with newly restored sight marvels over the beauty of his new world, so John could only talk incessantly of the glory of Christ. "He's higher, He's greater, He's more wonderful!"

As a Leader

Next, as one who preached repentance, baptized thousands, and amassed a group of loyal followers, John also qualified as a leader. And in that position he faced the temptation of exploiting others' ignorance, because the people truly did not know who he was. For example, in verse 19 a delegation of priests and Levites came and asked him, "Who are you?" But John resisted the temptation to use their ignorance for his own advantage.

> And he confessed, and did not deny, and he con-
> fessed, "I am not the Christ." (v. 20)

He also plainly answered that he was not Elijah nor the Prophet; but only a voice crying in the wilderness and a humble water-baptizer who wasn't worthy to untie his Master's shoe (vv. 21, 23, 26–27). With heartwarming humility, he turned the spotlight on Jesus and refused to take advantage of the people's ignorance.

As an Authority

Last, John was an authority—he had answers that even the religious authorities lacked. The temptation of this type of role is to hide one's own humanity. But John overcame this too, as evidenced by his humble admission that, at first, he didn't recognize Christ.

> "And I did not recognize Him, but in order that He
> might be manifested to Israel, I came baptizing in
> water." (v. 31)

He confesses this not just once but twice.

> "And I did not recognize Him, but He who sent me
> to baptize in water said to me, 'He upon whom you
> see the Spirit descending and remaining upon Him,
> this is the one who baptizes in the Holy Spirit.'"
> (vv. 33)

What an honest admission for an authority to make! Take a moment to let the meaning of this sink in. If you are in a position of authority, do you confess openly that you are still a learner, that there are things you are still ignorant of? Are you as willing to declare your struggles as your victories? Those who are truly humble are quick to say, like John, "I didn't recognize . . . I didn't know . . . I wasn't aware."

In Luke 7, John revealed even more of his frail humanity when, as a prisoner in Herod's dungeon and a prisoner of his own doubt, he sent two of his disciples racing to Jesus with a question: "Are You the Expected One, or do we look for someone else?" (v. 19b).

Like us, John didn't always understand God's ways. He stumbled. He abandoned hope. He lost confidence. But unlike us so many times, John was willing to admit the truth . . . struggles and all. He was willing to be transparent, honest, and vulnerable.

His responses to pride's snares concerning his roles as spokesperson, leader, and authority impart to us a second secret of humility: *Humble people have the ability to handle subtle temptations.* And the only way to do this is to be honest about your spiritual condition and be willing to divert praise to Christ.

The Public and Its Applause

Perhaps the most difficult phase of John's life involved the public and its applause. It's in this arena that humility can most easily wither and blow away.

John had his own congregation, his own disciples, his own crowds. This acclaim could have choked his humble spirit, yet he meekly spoke of another whose leadership they should follow. Consequently, however, he was preaching himself right out of his pulpit. Watch what happens in the following scene.

> Again the next day John was standing with two of his disciples, and he looked upon Jesus as He walked, and said, "Behold, the Lamb of God!" And the two disciples heard him speak, and they followed Jesus. (John 1:35–37)

John's own disciples began applauding another leader. And in another scene, Jesus and His disciples came to the same area in which John ministered—invaded his territory, so to speak. Shifting loyalties, the people flocked to Jesus instead of John to be baptized. The reporters sharpened their pencils. "This showdown is going to be front-page news!" How would John respond?

> John answered and said, "A man can receive nothing, unless it has been given him from heaven. You

yourselves bear me witness, that I said, 'I am not the Christ,' but, 'I have been sent before Him.' He who has the bride is the bridegroom; but the friend of the bridegroom, who stands and hears him, rejoices greatly because of the bridegroom's voice. And so this joy of mine has been made full." (3:27–29)[4]

John is only the best man at the wedding, and he rejoices at the success of Jesus, the Groom. This illustrates the third secret of humility: *The humble person has the vision to see God's hand in another's life and applaud it.* John Ruskin's words get to the heart of the matter.

I believe that the first test of a truly great man is his humility. I do not mean by humility, doubt of his own power. But really great men have a curious feeling that the greatness is not in them, but through them. And they see something divine in every other man and are endlessly, foolishly, incredibly merciful.[5]

As inspiring as John's example is so far, you may be saying to yourself, "This is all great, but how can I ever have the wisdom and strength to respond so humbly?" Well, don't give up on John's guidance yet! Because the answer is found in the next phase of his life, a phase that reveals the foundation of his humble house.

Humility and Its Basis

In the heart of the third chapter of John, we find seven words that give us John's credo, that summarize his philosophy of life.

"He must increase, but I must decrease." (v. 30)

These words—in that order, always together, and never taken as an option—give us the cardinal secret of humility: *a constant commitment to the increase of Christ and the decrease of self.* It is only on this foundation that we can build a humble life.

---

4. God's relationship to Israel, Jerusalem, and the church has often been likened to that of a bridegroom and his bride. For verses concerning Israel, see Jeremiah 3:1–10, Hosea 2:16–20, and Ezekiel 16. Concerning Jerusalem, see Isaiah 62:1–5 and Revelation 21:2, 9–10. Concerning the church, see 2 Corinthians 11:2, Ephesians 5:25–27, Revelation 19:7–9.

5. John Ruskin, in *Quote Unquote,* comp. Lloyd Cory (Wheaton, Ill.: SP Publications, Victor Books, 1977), p. 158.

Being totally committed to Christ's increase means acknowledging that He is supreme and that His image is more important than our own. But this doesn't mean revising our own image to look mousy or unkempt or piously nondescript. It just means letting our lives act as a frame that shows up the masterpiece . . . Jesus Christ. And a worthy frame isn't tarnished or dull, plain or cheap; yet neither is it so elaborate that it overpowers its picture. Instead, with subtle loveliness, it draws the observer's eyes to the beautiful work of art it displays.

Kate Wilkinson encapsulated John's attitude toward Christ in the familiar hymn, "May the Mind of Christ, My Savior." May her words of commitment be our prayer as God develops in us humility's sparkling gem.

> May the love of Jesus fill me,
> As the waters fill the sea;
> Him exalting, self abasing—
> This is victory.
>
> May His beauty rest upon me
> As I seek the lost to win,
> And may they forget the channel,
> Seeing only Him.[6]

 Living Insights

"He must increase."

These words of John do not refer to the increase of Jesus' divine abilities, for deity indwelt Him fully; nor do they refer to the increase of His authority, for even the wind obeyed Him; nor do they refer to the increase of His glory, for God's angels worshipped Him. Then what do these words refer to? *Our vision of His greatness.*

Most people spend their lives in a tunnel, looking at Christ as if He were a pinhole of light in the distance. Is that all He is—or is that merely all we see? The closer we come to Him, the bigger He seems to get. And the closer we come to the Light, the more our lives and our spirits are bathed in the light of His glory.

6. Kate B. Wilkinson, "May the Mind of Christ, My Savior," in *Hymns for the Family of God* (Nashville, Tenn.: Paragon Associates, 1976), no. 483.

To what degree do you see Jesus? Is He still a far-off light, or does His nearness fill your view? Take some time to study Him through the prism of the following passages, and meditate on His glory.

Hebrews 1:1–4 _____

_____

Colossians 1:15–19; 2:9 _____

_____

Revelation 5:6–14 _____

_____

 Living Insights

"I must decrease."

Ironically, those who strain at becoming humble, who try to engineer their own decrease, only call attention to themselves. Socrates once pithily mocked a man for dressing with ostentatious poverty: "I can see your vanity, Antisthenes, through the holes in your cloak."[7]

On the other hand, people who aspire to exalt Christ divert attention from themselves. Commentator Arthur W. Pink said, "The more I am occupied with Christ, the less shall I be occupied with myself. Humility is not the product of direct cultivation, rather it is a *by-product.*"[8]

The question, then, is not "How can I humble myself?" but "How can I occupy myself with Christ?" The following exercise will help you train for this new occupation.

1. I praise God for (a person) _____

   because _____

   _____

   _____

7. *The Little, Brown Book of Anecdotes,* ed. Clifton Fadiman (Boston, Mass.: Little, Brown and Co., 1985), p. 18.

8. Arthur W. Pink, *Exposition of the Gospel of John* (Grand Rapids, Mich.: Zondervan Publishing House, 1975), p. 149.

2. I praise God for (an undeserved blessing) _____

_____

_____

3. I praise God for (one of His qualities) _____

_____

_____

_____

_____

Rather than talking about yourself, your problems, or your circumstances, begin your trek toward humility by sharing these praises with someone today. Others will notice Christ increasing and not even realize that you are decreasing at the same time.

Chapter 4

A RIVER, A DOVE, A VOICE
Matthew 3:1–17

A young boy in India stands at the shore of a cold, dingy river. To enter the water and be baptized as a Christian will not only confirm his fledgling faith, but will also test it with fire. For when he comes up from the water he must face his Hindu family. They will consider him a traitor and an infidel. His father will never look at him or speak to him again. His mother will weep; his brothers will shake their fists. For this boy, baptism is a serious thing.

In our culture, though, baptism carries little of that social stigma. Fathers rarely get angry and mothers seldom weep when their child is baptized. In fact, for many baptism today has taken a backseat alongside church membership and the 10 percent tithe.

For Jesus, however, baptism carried great significance. His own baptism enlivened His ministry with power and authority,[1] and it confirmed His commitment to serve the Father even to death on a cross. And yet, in contrast to its regal importance, it required only the most common of elements—a river, a dove, and a voice.

The Baptizer's Predictions

Before Jesus' baptism, John sounded the alarm of God's approaching kingdom. The people crowded to hear him and be baptized because his message challenged them. It was simple, forthright, and courageous, unlike the mishmash of verbiage the Pharisees offered. He bluntly told them that their entrance into God's kingdom depended on heartfelt repentance, not on external religiosity or their Jewish lineage (see Matt. 3:7–9).

His messages also included predictions concerning the coming Messiah. We can identify four clear prophecies from the following passage:

> "As for me, I baptize you with water for repentance,
> but He who is coming after me is mightier than I,

---

1. At Jesus' baptism, He was granted special authority over the earthly and heavenly realms when the Father pronounced, "This is My beloved Son, in whom I am well-pleased" (Matt. 3:17b). He also received the power to act upon that divine authority from the Holy Spirit who came upon Him in the form of a dove (see v. 16).

and I am not fit to remove His sandals; He will baptize you with the Holy Spirit and fire. And His winnowing fork is in His hand, and He will thoroughly
clear His threshing floor; and He will gather His
wheat into the barn, but He will burn up the chaff
with unquenchable fire." (Matt. 3:11–12)

The coming Christ would *baptize, clean, gather,* and *burn up.*
These prophecies refer to Jesus' actions when He will recompense
the wicked and reward the righteous. That judgment process began
at His first appearance on earth and will culminate at His Second
Coming in the future.

His judgments are poignantly illustrated by the ancient practice
of threshing wheat, when farmers used a winnowing fork to toss
harvested grain into the wind. The light, useless chaff would blow
to the side to be burned later, while the heavier, valuable kernels
of wheat would fall to the ground and be gathered into the barn.
In using this imagery, John was predicting that the traditional,
man-made religion of the Pharisees would be burned away like the
useless chaff. But the Messiah's new message of gracious redemption
would bring blessing and protection to all who repented and believed.

These prophecies alerted the people to an ominous storm of
judgment brewing on the horizon and let them know that repentance was their only shelter. Understandably, John's words also in-
furiated the puffed-up Pharisees because they undermined their false
religiosity. John's message was bold, newfangled, and authoritative;
and, like revolutionary ideas today, it met inevitable resistance.

We, too, may encounter resistance when we propose new ideas
that challenge venerated but biblical traditions. It may result in an
ulcer-causing battle between pastors and boards, children and par-
ents, or teachers and administrations. But John's words of advice
would be, "Stand fast. Keep going. Hang tough."

The Messiah's Arrival

Despite his prophetic gift, John did not know whether the Christ
would come before twilight closed another day or whether His
arrival was weeks, possibly years away. But each rising sun revealed
him faithfully performing his tasks of warning, exhorting, convicting, and baptizing. As Philip Keller writes,

When the day came for Jesus to gently close the
door to His carpenter shop for the last time, He

knew exactly where to go. With firm footsteps and quiet determination He set off directly to see John. Following the winding roads from the hill country of Nazareth, He headed down into the burning heat of the Jordan Valley where John was baptizing in the running river.[2]

And, as if to highlight the simplicity of the scene, Matthew briefly notes,

> Then Jesus arrived from Galilee at the Jordan coming to John, to be baptized by him. (v. 13)

John's Reluctance

Edging His way through the crowd, Jesus silently slipped off His sandals and eased into the mucky river to be baptized. Can you imagine John's surprise? Jesus, the Son of God, wanted to be baptized. Trying in vain to dissuade Jesus, John said,

> "I have need to be baptized by You, and do You come to me?" (v. 14b)

To the crowds, John's reluctance must have been perplexing. This man who had stood toe-to-toe with the religious heavyweights trembled in reverance before an unknown carpenter. F. B. Meyer writes,

> He who had never quailed before monarch or people, directly he came in contact with Christ, cast the crown of his manhood at his feet, and shrank away. The eagle that had soared unhindered in mid-heaven seemed transfixed by a sudden dart, and fell suddenly, with a strange, low cry, at the feet of its Creator.[3]

Jesus' Response

In spite of John's reluctance, Jesus knew that His baptism was crucial. John did not fully understand the significance of what he was about to do, but Jesus reassured him,

---

2. W. Phillip Keller, *Rabboni* (Old Tappan, N.J.: Fleming H. Revell Co., Power Books, 1977), pp. 78–79.

3. F. B. Meyer, *John the Baptist* (reprint, Fort Washington, Pa.: Christian Literature Crusade, 1983), p. 72.

"Permit it at this time; for in this way it is fitting for us to fulfill all righteousness." (v. 15b)[4]

Suddenly John realized it was not him leading and Jesus following; it was he and Jesus *together,* somehow "fulfilling righteousness." F. B. Meyer again captures the transcendent meaning of this moment.

> And whenever some hesitant soul, timid and nervous to the last degree, dares to step out, and do what it believes to be the right thing because it is becoming, Jesus comes to it, enlinks his arm, and says, "Thou art not alone in this. Thou and I stand together here. It becomes *us* to fill up to its full measure all righteousness."[5]

So John agreed to baptize his Savior. His hesitation faded when his Master called him to obey.

The Baptism Itself

It took only a few seconds for Jesus to plunge into and come out of the murky water, but those few seconds bore a grand intensity. By comparing the accounts in Luke and Mark, we can follow what happened in slow motion.

Immersion in River

It was late in the day and many had already been baptized when Jesus entered the water (see Luke 3:21a). But Jesus' baptism was not like any of the others, as Mark writes:

> And immediately coming up out of the water, He saw the heavens opening, and the Spirit like a dove descending upon Him. (Mark 1:10)

Dove from Heaven

Luke describes the same event in his gospel, but he adds an element that Mark leaves out—as Jesus emerged from the water, He

---

4. How did Jesus' baptism "fulfill all righteousness"? We know that it wasn't for a show of repentance, for His heart was pure. Rather, Jesus approached the waters as the soon-to-be-sacrificed Lamb of God. Through baptism, Jesus identified Himself with the sinful people. Thus, He became the world's representative to later bear sin's judgment on the cross (see 2 Corinthians 5:21). For a thorough treatment of the reasons for Christ's baptism, see J. Dwight Pentecost's *The Words and Works of Jesus Christ* (Grand Rapids, Mich.: Zondervan Publishing House, 1981), pp. 92–95.

5. Meyer, *John the Baptist,* p. 75.

was talking to His Father. He saw the heavens tearing open as His eyes were lifted upward in prayer.

> And while He was praying, heaven was opened, and
> the Holy Spirit descended upon Him in bodily form
> like a dove. (Luke 3:21b–22a)

Luke is also more specific than Mark when he describes the dove. This dove was not merely a symbol of the Holy Spirit but actually was the Holy Spirit in bodily form, a theophany. Imagine John's astonishment as he saw the heavens parting, the Son of God praying, and the Holy Spirit descending. But that's not all.

Voice of God

To complete the presence of the Trinity, the Father made a pronouncement,

> And a voice came out of heaven, "Thou art My be-
> loved Son, in Thee I am well-pleased." (v. 22b)

This statement goes far beyond a fatherly pat on the head. It is a regal installment of Jesus as both the sovereign King (see Ps. 2:6–9) and the beneficent Servant-Savior (see Isa. 42:1–4). The baptism was finished, but Jesus' courageous mission as the Lamb of God had just begun.

The Practical Implications

In the few instants it took John to perform the baptism, an extraordinary transference occurred. From now until his death, John would decrease in influence, and Jesus would increase. Although unexpected and unorthodox, Jesus' baptism came at the right time, in the right way, and for the right reason, as we see in His words to John.

> "Permit it at this time; for in this way it is fitting for
> us to fulfill all righteousness." (Matt. 3:15)

These phrases—"at this time," "in this way," and "to fulfill all righteousness"—indicate three characteristics of God's sometimes unusual plans for us. Let's look at them a little more closely so that we, like John, may be inclined to submit and obey.

At This Time

The Lord's timing sometimes seems beyond reason, but if we could only see things as He does, we'd understand that it's divinely precise. Jesus' request for baptism definitely took John by surprise. But despite his confusion, he still understood that the timing was right and Jesus had to be obeyed.

Are you also feeling the Spirit's subtle prodding toward a sudden change of plans? Maybe from your perspective the timing seems off, but from God's viewpoint, it is perfect. Relax and permit the change, for the Lord will be glorified if you do.

In This Way

Sometimes God's ways of doing things don't seem to make sense. Just think about it. Does yelling at a wall make it crumble? It does if the wall is around Jericho. Do ninety-year-old women usually have babies? There was one who did—Sarah. And Saviors don't normally ask to be baptized, but the Son of God did, and it was the right way for His ministry to begin.

Has the Spirit's leading confused you lately? An unexpected change in career, an unforeseen short-term mission opportunity, or an unplanned pregnancy may be part of God's plan for you. It may be a chance to do something out of the ordinary for Him. Proceed in God's will, do it His way, and commit the outcome to Him.

To Fulfill All Righteousness

When we respond to God's will with obedience, we become intimately linked with Him in a work of righteousness. This step-by-step partnership may take us miles off the crowded highway and into an intimidating, uncharted forest. Alone, we would despair, but the reassurance of Christ's presence gives us the courage to press on. There in the lonely places God quiets the fears, takes care of the needs, and leads the way. Our part is to respond without reluctance and to surrender in obedience as, hand in hand, we walk with Jesus down God's narrow road.

 Living Insights

In 1850's Chicago, there was no better shoe salesman than D. L. Moody. A man with a racehorse spirit, he had a notion for riches, and nothing would—or could—stop him. Then, in the slums of Chicago's North Side, he met a few ragamuffin boys with names like Red Eye, Madden the Butcher, and Jackey Candles. Seeing their need for Jesus, Moody invited these young reprobates to Sunday school. But the stuffy classes soon bored these street-wise boys, so in an abandoned railroad freight car, Moody started his own Sunday school. Selling shoes suddenly seemed not so important.

Devoting every spare hour to reaching new recruits, this part-time Pied Piper felt God's call to abandon his booming shoe business and go into full-time Christian service. But it was no easy decision. "I fought against it. It was a terrible battle," Moody admitted.[6] It meant spending all his savings, living on crackers and cheese, rooming at the YMCA, and putting off marriage. It was a crazy call, and he wrestled with it for three sleepless months.

Similarly, John may have thought it was a crazy call when Jesus asked to be baptized. But Jesus simply said, "Permit it;" or, in today's terms, "Just do it."

What "crazy" thing might God be wanting you to do? Teaching even though you stutter? Using vacation time for a mission trip? Making pizzas for the junior high kids down the block? That's crazy! But God says, "Just do it." Write down what that "crazy" thing is and how it might be accomplished.

_____

_____

_____

_____

The rest of Moody's story? He did resign his sales job, and by age twenty-three his Sunday school had grown to about fifteen hundred children. Five years later he became president of the YMCA. And, by age fifty, this uneducated preacher had founded a Bible institute and evangelized thousands on two continents. A John the Baptizer type of man, this was "Crazy Moody."

 Living Insights STUDY TWO

Encountering Jesus while waist-deep in the sludgy Jordan River, John the Preparer, the Smoother, the Clearer, the Usher became, in a wink of an instant, the Preventer.

---

6. John Pollock, *Moody* (Chicago, Ill.: Moody Press, 1983), p. 51.

> Then Jesus arrived from Galilee at the Jordan
> coming to John, to be baptized by him. *But John tried
> to prevent Him.* (Matt. 3:13–14a, emphasis added)

Isn't that ironic? Until that moment, John's existence had been for the sole purpose of clearing the way for Jesus. Yet here—perhaps because of a momentary lapse of faith, or from the exhaustion of the day, or from the undeniable headiness of meeting the Son of God, or worse, because of the subtle invasion of humble-sounding pride—John was blocking the way.

Can you recall another incident in Scripture in which an ardent disciple stands in Jesus' way? Read Matthew 16:21–23. Who is the preventer in this scene? What is he trying to prevent?

_____

Why do you think Jesus' reaction is so vehement?

_____

_____

Why does Jesus address Satan? How is he involved?

_____

_____

Jesus accuses Satan of two things in verse 23. What are they?

1. _____

2. _____

Comparing this passage with Matthew 3:13–17, where Jesus confronts John, notice that the two events about which Jesus encounters resistance are His baptism and His crucifixion. But neither John, Peter, nor even death could keep Jesus from His determined objective—our salvation.

Have you been preventing Christ's influence in a certain situation? Pray silently regarding this matter. In your prayer acknowledge your resistance, submit your will, and permit His plan for your life.

Chapter 5

WHEN COMMITMENT LEADS TO MISTREATMENT

Mark 6:14–20; Matthew 11:1–3

With a plop, you toss your textbooks onto the small desk and sleepily settle into the cold plastic seat. Wiping the morning fog from your eyes, you take a look around to see a slow parade of fellow students shuffling into the classroom. Everybody has to take this class; it's mandatory—one of those classes they forgot to mention at freshman orientation.

"Know anything about the prof?" you ask your neighbor with the tousled hair.

"The toughest," he groans.

At that moment, the slope-shouldered professor stamps through the door, arriving at the lectern precisely as the bell rings. He takes a moment to allow a morgue-like silence to chill each student. Then, in a grating voice, he says,

"Welcome, freshmen, to the one course you can never drop, withdraw from, transfer out of, or ditch. In fact, my callow students, this is one class you'll remain in for the rest of your lives. In short . . . welcome to Mistreatment 101."

Mistreatment *Will* Occur: Count on It

Mistreatment is one of the few sure things in life, whether we're Christians or not. It's one of those dreaded courses that everyone must take. Don't believe that? Then turn to another of life's certainties—the Bible—where reality is never airbrushed and the truth never softened.

Scriptural Predictions

Jesus is the first to issue a mistreatment storm warning.

> "These things I have spoken to you, that in Me you may have peace. *In the world you have tribulation*, but take courage; I have overcome the world." (John 16:33, emphasis added)

What exactly does Jesus mean by *tribulation*? Flip back to verse 2 in the same chapter:

"They will make you outcasts from the synagogue,
but an hour is coming for everyone who kills you to
think that he is offering service to God."

Jesus doesn't paint a rosy picture for us, does He? Neither does the apostle Paul.

Indeed, all who desire to live godly in Christ Jesus
will be persecuted. (2 Tim. 3:12)

Often we think that godliness will shield us; but the truth is, the more the commitment, the more the persecution. As if that weren't bad enough, James goes on to promise trials.

Consider it all joy, my brethren, when you encounter various trials, knowing that the testing of
your faith produces endurance. (James 1:2–3)

Notice that James does not say "if," but gives us a definitive "when." Trials will buffet us as surely as wind follows winter.

Peter is next to join these plain-speaking prophets, assuring us of mistreatment's inevitability as he writes,

For what credit is there if, when you sin and are harshly
treated, you endure it with patience? But if when
you do what is right and suffer for it you patiently
endure it, this finds favor with God. (1 Pet. 2:20)

At first glance, it seems that Peter is saying, "If you do what is right and suffer for it . . ." But the "if" really belongs later in the sentence. What he's actually saying is this: "*When* you do what is right and suffer for it you will find favor only *if* you patiently endure it." Mistreatment will occur; that we can count on. But how we respond to it is the iffy part.

Human Reactions

How should we respond when mistreatment's pressure begins to build? Peter gives us the seldom-followed answer.

But even if you should suffer for the sake of righteousness, you are blessed. And do not fear their
intimidation, and do not be troubled. (1 Pet. 3:14)

38

Don't fear intimidation and don't be troubled. These are not natural responses! Even John the Baptizer struggled and wavered when mistreatment intruded on his life. Yet in the end, he managed to regain his equilibrium and stand firm in his faith. So let's take a look at his story and see what we can learn about facing intimidation and mistreatment . . . fearlessly.

Mistreatment Did Occur: A Classic Example

If it were true that good people are exempt from mistreatment, then John would have been exempt, for he was a remarkably good man.

John's Life and Commitment

Jesus recognized the quality of John's life in Matthew 11:7–11a.

> And as these were going away, Jesus began to speak to the multitudes about John, "What did you go out into the wilderness to look at? A reed shaken by the wind? But what did you go out to see? A man dressed in soft clothing? Behold, those who wear soft clothing are in kings' palaces. But why did you go out? To see a prophet? Yes, I say to you, and one who is more than a prophet. This is the one about whom it is written,
> 'Behold, I send My messenger before
>   Your face,
> Who will prepare Your way before You.'
> Truly, I say to you, among those born of women there has not arisen anyone greater than John the Baptist."

Here was a man who was pure in motive, single-minded in purpose, simple in lifestyle. He was unpretentious and humble—a man of strong convictions. He was unmoved by peer pressure and absolutely correct in his vision of the world in which he lived. Yet, in spite of the quality of his character, mistreatment occurred. John was unjustly sent to prison.

Things That Triggered the Treatment

How could an innocent man like John end up in jail? The gospels tell us about two conditions that rattled the cell keys in Herod's pocket. The first was that *John became too popular with the people.* Although this is not directly stated in the gospels, we can see it implied in a scene that followed John's death.

> And King Herod heard of it [Jesus' miracles], for His name had become well known; and people were saying, "John the Baptist has risen from the dead, and that is why these miraculous powers are at work in Him." But others were saying, "He is Elijah." And others were saying, "He is a prophet, like one of the prophets of old." But when Herod heard of it, he kept saying, "John, whom I beheaded, has risen!" (Mark 6:14–16)

As Jesus became more well known, people began linking Him to John, whom Herod had killed. John the Baptizer had won the people's allegiance through impeccable scruples and courageous honesty. The masses knew the filth that lay underneath Herod's rich veneer, and seeing the comparison, they turned away from him in disgust. Because of John's popularity, Herod felt he had no choice but to imprison him.

The second condition, then, was that *John declared the truth too openly*. And this made mendacious Herod squirm. Verses 17–20 reveal the story.

> For Herod himself had sent and had John arrested and bound in prison on account of Herodias, the wife of his brother Philip, because he had married her. For John had been saying to Herod, "It is not lawful for you to have your brother's wife." And Herodias had a grudge against him and wanted to put him to death and could not do so; for Herod was afraid of John, knowing that he was a righteous and holy man, and kept him safe. And when he heard him, he was very perplexed; but he used to enjoy listening to him.

The injustice of John's imprisonment disturbs us. What crime had John committed? There was nothing wrong in being popular or in pointing out the truth. But, like Jesus, John suffered because of his righteousness.

His Mental and Emotional Anguish

In the belly of a dank dungeon where hopes rot and dreams disappear, John was consumed by the emotional blackness. William Barclay describes the scene.

For any man that would have been a terrible fate, but for John the Baptist it was worse than for most men. He was the child of the desert; all his life he had lived in the wide open spaces, with the clean wind on his face and the spacious vault of the sky for his roof. And now he was confined within the four narrow walls of an underground dungeon. For a man like John, who had probably never lived in a house, this must have been an agony.[1]

Like the rags he wore, John's once robust spirit began to tatter. Doubt pierced his mind, and he began asking himself, "Why is Jesus waiting to initiate the kingdom?. . . Could it be Jesus is a false Christ?. . . Is my whole life a waste?. . . Will I die for nothing?" Finally, he could bear it no longer and sent word to Jesus.

> Now when John in prison heard of the works of Christ, he sent word by his disciples, and said to Him, "Are You the Expected One, or shall we look for someone else?" (Matt. 11:2–3)

This great, holy, courageous man was beginning to crumble under mistreatment's merciless fist.

You, like John, may be experiencing the despair of the dungeon. You've been honest, you've done what was right—yet wrong has resulted. A door has slammed shut and trapped you with only fears and doubts for company. If a man like John couldn't keep from breaking down, how will people like us be able to stand firm?

When Mistreatment Does Occur: Some Suggestions

Whatever the circumstances of your mistreatment, there is hope. The following principles can help you hang tough and see you through to the other side.

First: *Consider the source.* When someone who lives in the wrong does you wrong, well, that's natural, now isn't it? And if it's someone who thought he or she was doing right, it helps to remember that. Putting ourselves in the other person's shoes will keep us from sinking into bitterness.

---

1. William Barclay, *The Gospel of Matthew,* vol. 2, 2d ed., The Daily Study Bible series (Philadelphia, Pa.: Westminster Press, 1958), pp. 1–2.

Second: *Focus on the truth.* It is comforting to know that what brought on the mistreatment was truth; being in the right is a great source of confidence. Another source of strength is remembering that God has not abandoned His truth . . . nor has He abandoned us.

Third: *Watch your attitude.* When we've been hurt, it's easy to let feelings of self-pity, bitterness, or resentment creep in. And it's easy to want to hurl blame, to panic, to get revenge. Sometimes we feel hatred—even toward God. But these attitudes can derail us from our goal of serving Christ. Instead of letting them take over, we need to accept the prison experience as part of God's plan for us and continue to serve Him in the midst of it.

Fourth: *Stay in touch with objective, spiritually-minded companions.* Although John was alone in the dungeon, he still had contact with his disciples. Companions in mistreatment are like two soldiers in the trenches—enduring the pummeling of the enemy's bombs together, they keep each other sane and hopeful.

Fifth: *Seize the setback as an opportunity for growth, rather than a detour into the flatlands of doubt.* Let's turn again to Peter's counsel on this subject.

> In this you greatly rejoice, even though now for a little while, if necessary, you have been distressed by various trials, that the proof of your faith, being more precious than gold which is perishable, even though tested by fire, may be found to result in praise and glory and honor at the revelation of Jesus Christ. (1 Pet. 1:6–7)

We're gold in the making! Keeping that perspective can revolutionize our attitude toward unjust treatment. Through the endurance and maturity we develop in the smelting pot of mistreatment, we become worthy showpieces for Christ. Scott Peck writes in *The Road Less Traveled,*

> What makes life difficult is that the process of confronting and solving problems is a painful one. . . .
> Yet it is in this whole process of meeting and solving problems that life has its meaning. Problems are the cutting edge that distinguishes between success and failure. Problems call forth our courage and our wisdom; indeed, they create our courage and our

wisdom. It is only because of problems that we grow mentally and spiritually.[2]

And remember, John Bunyan titled his classic allegory *Pilgrim's Progress*, not *Pilgrim's Destination*. For in the story, Christian trekked up and down, up and down on his seesawing spiritual journey. We, too, are on a journey—growing, stretching, progressing. Invariably, we will meet with mistreatment. But rather than fear it, let's profit from its valuable lessons so that one day God will greet us with a "Well done" embrace and a well-deserved reward.

 ## Living Insights

STUDY ONE

Many of you who are reading this are battle weary. Fighting enemies on all sides, you feel abandoned, ridiculed, victimized, empty. Your battle may be with an estranged family member or an irate neighbor. It may be in a courtroom, in a PTA meeting, or, of all places, in your church. Each is a different situation, but all have a common element. You did what was right, you were acting upon your commitment to Christ, and yet the whole thing backfired!

What is your battle? Take a moment to write down some of the details. Who is involved? What did you do? How did they respond?

In such a difficult battle, the natural response by even the most temperate person can be retaliation, revenge, or even rage. Don't worry, such feelings are normal—yes, even for Christians. But you do need a plan to handle your emotions because they can quickly tear you apart.

Author Ross West gives valuable advice on handling your anger. Picture your rage as a ball thrown at you by the one who has mistreated you. Now that you have this anger-ball, what can you

---

2. M. Scott Peck, *The Road Less Traveled* (New York, N.Y.: Simon and Schuster, A Touchstone Book, 1978), p. 16.

do with it? You can swallow it, but that might make you sick. You can throw it at someone else, but that destroys valuable friendships. You could play catch with it by talking about your anger with someone you trust. But in the end, you still go home with this wretched ball in your hands. Some people take the ball and "score" with it, channeling their anger into frantic productivity. But working harder to release pent-up anger can lead to burnout.

Well, what are you to do with this burdensome ball of anger? West counsels you to

> take it to the edge of the sea, place the ball in the hands of God, and let Him cast it as far away as the east is from the west, so that it sinks into the depths, never to be seen or heard from again.[3]

Won't you place your burden of anger and resentment in God's capable hands? In return, He will give you another ball—a helium-filled balloon called joy.

 Living Insights

Maybe your mistreatment has only been threatening. Do you see a foreboding storm of mistreatment forming on the horizon? Do the signs say, "Brace yourself. Here comes the big one"? The Lord revealed to the Old Testament prophet Habakkuk the menacing thunderclouds of the Babylonian invasion long before it happened. But although Habakkuk faced the future with fear, he also mustered a remarkable faith in God. Notice how Habakkuk expressed his fears in the following verse:

> Though the fig tree should not blossom,
> And there be no fruit on the vines,
> Though the yield of the olive should fail,
> And the fields produce no food,
> Though the flock should be cut off from the fold,
> And there be no cattle in the stalls . . .
> (Habakkuk 3:17)

The Babylonians were coming with pulverizing fury to destroy and annihilate. Nothing would be safe.

---

3. Ross West, *How to Be Happier in the Job You Sometimes Can't Stand* (Nashville, Tenn.: Broadman Press, 1990), p. 54.

What about your future? What is the worst that could happen? Could you lose your house? Could you lose your job? Could you lose a friendship? Write down all the bleak possibilities.

I could _____

I could _____

I could _____

I could _____

I could _____

These catastrophic "I coulds" are what haunt our sleepless nights and drive our grim imaginations. Yet in the most disastrous scenario, you must commit yourself to trusting God. Read what follows Habakkuk's list of woes . . . a beautiful statement of trust in God.

> Yet I will exult in the Lord,
> I will rejoice in the God of my salvation.
> The Lord God is my strength,
> And He has made my feet like hinds' feet,
> And makes me walk on my high places.
> (vv. 18–19)

Take time now to write down your own personal commitment to trust in God, using the same form as Habakkuk's prayer. May God place you back on the high road of praising and serving Him.

Yet, I will _____

I will _____

The Lord God is _____

And He has _____

And He will _____

Chapter 6

A DANCE OF DEATH

Mark 6:17–29

W hat man can live and not see death?" (Ps. 89:48a).

Reluctantly, we must answer the psalmist's question, "No one." Death awaits every man and woman—with no exceptions. Death never bargains for time, never shares its mysteries, and seldom happens the way we expect. Its perplexing ironies keep it distant and shadowy, shrouded from our understanding.

The death of John the Baptizer illuminates these dark truths. A man of noble and virtuous character, John should have met death heroically, perhaps on a glorious mission. Ironically, though, he died in a dreary dungeon at the whim of a lecherous despot who was enticed by a young girl's dance.

Ironic Facts about Death

When we think about death, at least three ironies seem to emerge again and again.

First: *Although death is sure, its arrival is usually sudden and surprising.* Each of us knows that death could be at the door any moment; yet when we hear its knock, we are startled and shocked. Its finality jolts us, forcing us to stand face-to-face with ultimate reality.

Second: *The way a person dies is occasionally the opposite of the way that person lived.* A man living a tranquil life may die violently. A once-loved celebrity may die forgotten and alone. A rich entrepreneur may die penniless. Death is no respecter of persons, nor does the way in which it comes respect the tenor of a person's life.

Third: *Rather than silencing a person's life, death often underscores it.* Death is not always a period; sometimes it is an exclamation point. For instance, a tyrant may try to silence his opponent by killing him, but this only makes the martyr's followers proclaim his ideals all the louder. Indeed, the voices of martyred missionaries have been heard by many more after their death than before, inspiring countless others to take their place in the fight.

These ironic facts about death stand true in John the Baptizer's case as well. John was probably shocked to see the executioner's shadow at his door. Although he knew death could come at any time, he probably believed that Herod was too fearful and weak to order his execution. John's death also stood in stark contrast to his life. A simple man from the desert, he should have died naturally and honorably. Yet he was wrongfully imprisoned and unjustly executed. Finally, although Herod had hoped to quiet John's influence by killing him, he actually amplified it. His death brings out the wickedness of Herod's court in bold relief, and it challenges us to be equally courageous as we face the Herods of our world.

Having described John's death in general terms, let's now look at the specifics. How and why was John murdered?

John's Death: How and Why

The details of John's death are complicated and disturbing. It happened in a vicious culture that is foreign to us in more than one way. It was a time when entertainment often included gore and death; a time when a king's whim could cost a man his head. And such was John's fate, whose story is unravelled in Mark 6:17–29.

Herod and Herodias: A Marriage

The first thread we must trace through this dark fabric is the sordid marriage of Herod and Herodias,[1] which John denounced.

> For Herod himself had sent and had John arrested and bound in prison on account of Herodias, the wife of his brother Philip, because he had married her. For John had been saying to Herod, "It is not lawful for you to have your brother's wife." And Herodias had a grudge against him and wanted to put him to death and could not do so. (Mark 6:17–19)

Herod had married Herodias, who was his niece as well as the wife of his stepbrother, Herod Philip. According to the Scriptures, it was strictly forbidden for a man to marry his brother's wife (Lev. 20:21).[2] This immoral relationship was only one grain of filth in a

1. Herodias was the sister of Agrippa I who had close ties to the Imperial family in Rome. John the Baptist had great courage to stand up to such a powerful and influential woman.

2. A man could marry his brother's wife if his brother died without an heir. This was called a levirate marriage (Deut. 25:5–6). Herod Philip should not be confused with Philip the Tetrarch who controlled the region northeast of Galilee. Herod Philip was struck from the will of his father, Herod the Great, and did not rule any regions in Palestine. He married his niece, Herodias, the daughter of his brother, Aristobulus, who was strangled to death by command of his father in 7 B.C.

47

family with a foul heritage. Herod's father, Herod the Great, took control of Palestine in 37 B.C. after slaying thousands of Jews. During his thirty-four-year reign, he married at least ten women with whom he lived in polygamy. He executed one wife, one mother-in-law, two brothers-in-law, three sons, and anyone else who opposed him. It was said, "It is safer to be Herod's pig than Herod's son."[3]

As a teenager, Herod was promised his father's throne, but instead he received tetrach status as a subordinate ruler around the Sea of Galilee. His brother, Archelaus, inherited kingship in Jerusalem and promptly carried on his father's reign of terror among the Jews.

In contrast to the vicious immorality of the Herodian court, John the Baptizer stood as a beacon of purity, exposing the evil rulers of his day. For this stand, he was imprisoned and finally executed.

John and Herod: A Rebuke

John's rebuke of Herod's corrupt marriage is the second thread in the story. When he indicted the immoral couple, he was not only insulting and embarrassing them, but he was also sowing the seeds of a political nightmare. Since the Baptizer was immensely popular and influential, his statements could have fueled a rebellion that would have damaged Herod and Herodias' reputation in Rome and paralyzed their plans for more power. So in response, Herodias—who was more ambitious than her husband—seethed with hatred for John, while Herod was strangely attracted to him in spite of his potential threat.

> For Herod was afraid of John, knowing that he was a righteous and holy man, and kept him safe. And when he heard him, he was very perplexed; but he used to enjoy listening to him. (Mark 6:20)

Herod feared John, but he also feared his wife—who was a conniving and power-hungry Jezebel. Caught between his conscience and his contentious wife, he imprisoned John to protect him from Herodias but also to keep him nearby.

Herod's Birthday: A Dance

The third thread is the most heinous, for it was the bait that set Herodias' vengeful trap in motion. Herodias had been patiently

---

3. See Paul Barnett's book *Behind the Scenes of the New Testament* (Downers Grove, Ill.: InterVarsity Press, 1990), pp. 20–24. Herod was half Jewish and would not have eaten pork, so his pigs were safer than his sons.

waiting for just the right moment when her husband would be vulnerable enough to agree to her deadly designs.

> And a strategic day came when Herod on his birthday gave a banquet for his lords and military commanders and the leading men of Galilee. (v. 21)

Did you notice the word *strategic?* This word reveals the wheels of cruelty turning in Herodias' treacherous mind. For she knew that her husband had two main weaknesses, lust and pride. So at his birthday banquet, she assembled these ingredients to subdue Herod's will and concoct her revenge. While Herod and his pals were reveling unrestrained, she sent her teenage daughter from her previous marriage into the room to dance seductively before her stepfather. Lust filled Herod's eyes and pride filled his heart, and in an attempt to impress his locker-room buddies, he made a foolish promise to the girl.

> And when the daughter of Herodias herself came in and danced, she pleased Herod and his dinner guests; and the king said to the girl, "Ask me for whatever you want and I will give it to you." And he swore to her, "Whatever you ask of me, I will give it to you; up to half of my kingdom." (vv. 22–23)

Thus, Herod rashly and blindly offered Herodias her chance to call for John's execution. A dance of sin ironically turned into a dance of death for the virtuous Baptizer.

John's Deathday: A Tragedy

As Herod fell to temptation, the sordid tapestry was complete. Upon hearing his oath, the girl ran to Herodias and returned with the grim wish.

> And she went out and said to her mother, "What shall I ask for?" And she said, "The head of John the Baptist." And immediately she came in haste before the king and asked, saying, "I want you to give me right away the head of John the Baptist on a platter." (vv. 24–25)

Herod's lust had lured him into the trap, and now his pride bound him helpless. A night of revelry turned sour as Herod, a fool who would not risk his manly image and recant his oath, ordered the execution of John the Baptizer.

And although the king was very sorry, yet because of his oaths and because of his dinner guests, he was unwilling to refuse her. And immediately the king sent an executioner and commanded him to bring back his head. And he went and had him beheaded in the prison, and brought his head on a platter, and gave it to the girl; and the girl gave it to her mother. (vv. 26–28)

Because one man fell to temptation, tragic consequences occurred. We can shake our heads with disgust and contempt for Herod, but are we really so different? We, too, fall to temptation when we become absorbed in ourselves and our pleasures. We may not deliberately turn our backs on God; we just sort of forget Him, unconsciously unplugging ourselves from His power. Herod's sorrow and the gruesome image of John's death should be a reminder to us of the painful consequences of succumbing to temptation.

Timely Observations

Without warning, without reason, without dignity, John died because of a frivolous boast by a self-indulgent potentate who was enticed by an impudent teenager. As sad as his death was, the injustice and irony of it is even more upsetting. In the context of such a tragedy, we can be reminded of four principles.

First: *When right confronts wrong, retaliation often occurs.* Right will never win uncontested. Just as in John's case, evil will fight back unscrupulously. It does not remain dormant, and it will not just go away. We must learn to expect and prepare for this retaliation.

Second: *When weakness and wickedness clash, wickedness wins.* Herod was a man of weak character and, therefore, was easy prey for Herodias' wicked plot. Wickedness will triumph when we are weak, so we must be vigilant in pursuing spiritual strength. Worship services, Christian fellowship, spirit-enriching retreats, prayer, and Scripture memorization are vital aspects of a spiritually fit lifestyle.

Third: *When decisions are made in a context of lust, they bring bitter consequences.* The night began with playful lust, but it ended in murder. Herod had only planned to enjoy his birthday; but when he celebrated his lust instead, he was left with bitter, recurring remorse for the murder of an innocent man. Sin never starts out tasting bitter; it starts out sweet as the fruit in the Garden of Eden. But when it takes root in our lives, it brings only destruction and shame.

Fourth: *When death precedes repentance, guilt haunts the living.* Herod was haunted by his guilt, for when he heard of Jesus' miracles, he feared that Jesus was actually John come back from the dead.

> And King Herod heard of it, for His name had become well known; and people were saying, "John the Baptist has risen from the dead, and that is why these miraculous powers are at work in Him." But others were saying, "He is Elijah." And others were saying, "He is a prophet, like one of the prophets of old." But when Herod heard of it, he kept saying, "John, whom I beheaded, has risen!" (vv. 14–16)

Notice that Herod "*kept* saying." He could find no rest from the guilt that rifled through his mind.

Although the death of John the Baptizer is disquieting for its glaring injustice, we notice that, like his life, it was a protest against sin. His barb-like presence will be forever in our minds, spurring us to recognize our sin and return to faithful obedience.

"Though he is dead, he still speaks" (Heb. 11:4b).

 ## Living Insights

Dietrich Bonhoeffer was a twentieth-century John the Baptizer. With the same fury and determination as John, Bonhoeffer hurled lightning bolts of truth at a tyrannical despot whose cruelty surpassed even Herod's. Bonhoeffer's nemesis—Adolf Hitler.

Long before the public began to loathe Hitler, Bonhoeffer denounced him and his Nazism. In 1939 Bonhoeffer turned down a teaching position in the United States and joined the Resistance in Germany instead. Discovering his subversion, Hitler had him executed at the Flossenburg concentration camp only days before it was liberated by Allied troops.

Surely the safety and comforts of America were tempting to Bonhoeffer, but he found the strength to follow God even if that meant martyrdom. We would be wise to learn from his insights concerning temptation.

> Satan does not here fill us with hatred of God, but with forgetfulness of God. . . . The lust thus aroused

envelops the mind and will of man in deepest darkness. The powers of clear discrimination and of decision are taken from us.[4]

Take a moment to think about what kinds of temptation you face most often.

☐ Desire for possessions

☐ Angry impatience

☐ Lustful thoughts

☐ Lazy overindulgence

☐ Boastful pride

☐ Faithless fear

☐ Envy of others

As Bonhoeffer said, we do not succumb to these temptations because we hate God—we just forget Him. We forget to include Him in our daily routine, in our work schedule, in our out-of-town trips, in our living room, in our private moments. As we abandon God in these aspects of our lives, we are vulnerable to the power of the flesh and fall to temptation. Scripture gives us crucial commands in these situations. Read the following verses and write down these commands.

1 Corinthians 6:18 _____

2 Timothy 2:22 _____

_____

Bonhoeffer aptly summarizes God's word to us:

> Therefore the Bible teaches us in times of temptation in the flesh to *flee*. . . . Every struggle against lust in one's own strength is doomed to failure. Flee— that can indeed only mean, Flee to that place where you find protection and help, flee to the Crucified.[5]

---

4. Dietrich Bonhoeffer, *Creation and Fall / Temptation* (New York, N.Y.: Macmillan Publishing Co., Collier Books, 1959), pp. 116–17.

5. Bonhoeffer, *Creation and Fall / Temptation*, pp. 117–18.

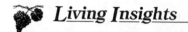 **Living Insights**

Dietrich Bonhoeffer advised us to flee from lust and "flee to the Crucified." How can we do this? The answer is in Romans 8:5–7. Read these verses and compare those who are of the "flesh" and of the "Spirit" by answering the following questions.

How can those who are "according to the flesh" and those who are "according to the Spirit" be identified?

_____

_____

What are the results of the two different mind-sets?

_____

What is the fleshly mind-set incapable of doing?

_____

_____

From these verses, we see that fleeing from temptation and fleeing to Christ is accomplished through our mind-set. If our thoughts are focused on the Cross, there will be power; if they are focused on our flesh, there will be failure. Bonhoeffer describes this focus and the power that will result.

> His image and his presence alone can help. Here we see the crucified body and perceive in it the end of all desire; here we see right through Satan's deceit and here our spirit again becomes sober and aware of the enemy. Here I perceive the forsakenness and abandonment of my fleshly condition and the righteous judgement of God's wrath on all flesh. Here I know that in this lost condition I could never have helped myself against Satan, but that it is the victory of Jesus Christ which I now share.[6]

6. Bonhoeffer, _Creation and Fall / Temptation_, p. 118.

Chapter 7

HE, BEING DEAD,
STILL SPEAKS

Selected Scripture

I never met a man I didn't like." . . . "We have nothing to fear but fear itself." . . . "Give me liberty, or give me death." . . . "Never give in, never give in, never, never, never, never."[1]

These words, though spoken by men who have long been dead, still encourage, inspire, and fill us with hope. This is especially true of heroes of the Christian faith. Jim Elliot, for example, was murdered while attempting to communicate the gospel to the violent Auca Indians in Ecuador. Yet, through time's long tunnel since his death, his words still reverberate loud and clear: "He is no fool who gives what he cannot keep to gain what he cannot lose."[2]

By the same token, however, words also have the power to leave a legacy of destruction. The father who derides his son, calling him a worthless bum or a lazy good-for-nothing, can scar him emotionally for years to come. Words such as these hit like exploding shrapnel, impairing and crippling the inner being. An entire lifetime can be spent attempting to soothe the sting and repair the damage.

Why do words affect us so? How can they have such power over us?

Perhaps the power is not in the words themselves, but in the person who speaks them. Words are able to breathe and feel and grab hold of us only because they dance on the lips of a person we revere. Truly, a life speaks louder than words . . . but words also can live forever because of a life.

In our study of John the Baptizer, we have considered many of his words. But we have also settled down next to him and grown close to him emotionally. His cries of doubt have reached our ears; his passion for Christ has stirred our hearts; his painful death has pricked fears in us that we did not know we had. His life and his words have touched us deeply. As it was said of Abel, it is also true of John, "Though he is dead, he still speaks" (Heb. 11:4b).

1. Attributed respectively to Will Rogers, Franklin D. Roosevelt, Patrick Henry, Winston Churchill.

2. Jim Elliot, as quoted by Elisabeth Elliot in *Shadow of the Almighty: The Life and Testament of Jim Elliot* (New York, N.Y.: Harper and Brothers, Publishers, 1958), p. 15.

Enduring Lines from John's Lips

The Baptizer speaks to us in many ways. His words impact us when he blasts the hypocrites, rebukes royalty, corrects sinners, and pales before Christ. His enduring model of faith teaches us several lessons vital to our spiritual growth.

Urgency

First, John was nothing if not urgent about his mission. His message of repentance raced out of the desert like an express train; those who didn't climb aboard would have the kingdom of heaven pass them by. As Isaiah had prophesied, John passionately cried in the wilderness:

> "Repent, for the kingdom of heaven is at hand."
> (Matt. 3:2; see also Luke 3:3–6)

John had a driving vision of God's purpose for his life. He was a man with a burning message, and there was no time to wait, no time to get sidetracked—only time to tell one more person to get ready.

Simplicity

John was a man of profound understanding, yet he knew how to keep his message simple. The other teachers of his day were confusing and frustrating; the people must have often felt they were lost in a religious house of mirrors. But John's words were practical, to the point, and easy to understand. For example, look how he told them to demonstrate their repentance.

> "Let the man who has two tunics share with him
> who has none; and let him who has food do like-
> wise." (Luke 3:11b)

The people were used to hearing complicated treatises that analyzed the kind of sin, the day of the offense, the persons involved, and the required sacrifices. John just said, "It's simple. Love your neighbor."

We can be just as guilty of muddling God's plain truth. Gerhard E. Frost writes about this in his poem "Haunting Words."

> When I think of teaching
> I recall another teacher's words:
> "If you can't say it simply,
> you either don't understand it
> or you don't believe it."

Haunting words,
but are they true?

Yes, when you believe,
and try to say what you believe,
knowledge weds wisdom
and heart-language is born.
Little words, feeling words,
sturdy, simple words,
strong-backed servants
emerge to do Truth's bidding,
for simplicity is the vocabulary
of depth.[3]

Don't mistake confusion for depth. Simple words spoken passionately from the soul are deep. Those kinds of words command attention, draw crowds, and change lives.

As we grow older, let's grow simpler and wiser too. Maturity in Christ is not measured by intricate and lofty public prayers, nor is it calculated by the number of theological words we dispense. Rather, maturity flowers as we clear away the verbal weeds and live by the simple truths of Scripture.

Authenticity

John's authenticity also speaks to us. He always stood firm on the subjects of sin, repentance, and the superiority of Christ—whether he was on friendly ground or hostile. He was true to his calling and honest about his role in every situation.

For a look at his authenticity in action, read his truthful response to the priests and Levites who had been sent by the Pharisees to find out who he was.[4]

And he confessed, and did not deny, and he confessed, "I am not the Christ." And they asked him,

3. Excerpted from Gerhard E. Frost's poem, "Haunting Words," reprinted from the January 1979 issue of *Parish Teacher,* © 1979, Augsburg Publishing House. Used by permission of Augsburg Fortress.

4. The Pharisees, offended by John, commissioned a delegation of priests to scrutinize the son of Zacharias, their fellow Levite. They meant to discredit him, hoping he would make a false claim to be the Messiah or one of the prophets. But John eluded their trap with his authentic confession and, in turn, exposed their own foolishness. For the Christ stood right in their midst, and they did not even recognize Him (vv. 25–26). As commentator William Hendriksen noted, "In their search for false Messiahs they have missed the true One." (A *Commentary on the Gospel of John* [London, England: Banner of Truth Trust, 1954], p. 97).

"What then? Are you Elijah?" And he said, "I am not." "Are you the Prophet?" And he answered, "No." They said then to him, "Who are you, so that we may give an answer to those who sent us? What do you say about yourself?" He said, "I am a voice of one crying in the wilderness, 'Make straight the way of the Lord,' as Isaiah the prophet said." (John 1:20–23)

In another instance, John modeled authenticity before his loyal disciples when he told them straight out that Christ was the Messiah, not he.

The next day he saw Jesus coming to him, and said, "Behold, the Lamb of God who takes away the sin of the world!" (v. 29)

The Pharisees and Sadducees did not escape the sharp side of John's authenticity, as we can see in John's forthright confrontation of their hypocrisy.

"You brood of vipers, who warned you to flee from the wrath to come? Therefore bring forth fruit in keeping with repentance; and do not suppose that you can say to yourselves, 'We have Abraham for our father'; for I say to you, that God is able from these stones to raise up children to Abraham. And the axe is already laid at the root of the trees; every tree therefore that does not bear good fruit is cut down and thrown into the fire." (Matt. 3:7b–10)

Even in the company of royalty, John did not swerve from his straight and narrow calling. Remember his blunt rebuke of Herod?

"It is not lawful for you to have your brother's wife." (Mark 6:18b)

Whether with friends or foes, the powerful or the obscure, John remained true to himself and his Lord. Though pressured to alter his lines, he sounded them loud and clear. And he remained authentic and honest to the day of his death.

There's something magnetic about real people like John. We want to be with them because they have no duplicity, no deceit, no hypocrisy. They set us at ease because we know where they stand. And even though we may not like what they say, we are willing to listen because we know they mean what they say.

Purity

Purity, another enduring quality of John's, was recognized, ironically, by Herod—the most impure person in John's story. Mark writes,

> Herod was afraid of John, knowing that he was a righteous and holy man, and kept him safe. And when he heard him, he was very perplexed; but he used to enjoy listening to him. (6:20)

In comparison to his own corrupt soul, Herod saw that John was "a righteous and holy man." This not only intrigued Herod, it attracted him; and he enjoyed stepping out of his own sinful cesspool to be near John.

People with purity have that kind of effect on us as well. Like a cold splash in the face, their ethics invigorate us. They revive our hope that we, too, can experience freedom from guilt and be clean before God.

Humility

Finally, John's humility calls to us across the centuries. When Jesus began baptizing and teaching in John's neighborhood, the Baptizer did not competitively retaliate or scornfully sulk. Instead, he rejoiced!

> "He who has the bride is the bridegroom; but the friend of the bridegroom, who stands and hears him, rejoices greatly because of the bridegroom's voice. And so this joy of mine has been made full." (John 3:29)

Then the Baptizer makes a pronouncement that has become the grand synopsis of his life.

> "He must increase, but I must decrease." (v. 30)

In the course of your life, you may rise to higher levels of admiration and respect than you ever imagined possible. Yours may be the name dropped at socials, the advice sought by admiring followers, the solo voice of comfort and hope in your office, neighborhood, or school. But if you are not careful, an authoritative headiness may intoxicate your good sense . . . and you may forget that a humble voice is all you are.

Those Same Issues Apply Today

To the seminary-green pastor and the wise old pillar of the parish, the Baptizer's life shouts these golden admonitions:

- *Be urgent!* It will guard you from complacency.

- *Be simple!* It will help you cope with these complex and confusing times.

- *Be authentic!* It will enable you to resist hypocrisy.

- *Be pure!* It will sensitize you to the subtle forms of wrong in your heart.

- *Be humble!* It will check your pride and keep you easy to live with.

Though John now rests silent alongside history's other heroes, his virtuous qualities—urgency, simplicity, authenticity, purity, and humility—live on. May we learn from his timeless words and actions and have these enduring qualities live on in us as well!

 ## *Living Insights* STUDY ONE

If we were to take a magnifying glass to John the Baptizer's life, we would be amazed at how purely and clearly God's timeless truths stand out. If *he* were to take a magnifying glass to *our* lives, however, how clearly would he be able to see these same truths?

Developing a character like John's takes concentrated effort and much time. But don't be discouraged. God wants this for us even more than we want it for ourselves, and in His strength we can accomplish it. Let's take the first step today by beginning to act out one of John's enduring characteristics in Study One and another in Study Two. Let's start with the quality of *urgency*.

The Baptizer was not frantic; he was urgent. He was urgent because he knew what was of utmost importance, and he determined to invest more energy and sweat in that area than any other. This urgency effectively kept him safeguarded against a costly characteristic—complacency.

Complacency comes from choosing to be ignorant regarding what is important and being satisfied with inactivity. *Webster's* defines it as "self-satisfaction accompanied by unawareness of actual dangers or deficiencies."[5] In contrast, John knew the grave spiritual dangers that awaited those who rejected Christ, and he was also aware of the spiritual deficiency among the people he loved. And,

---

5. *Webster's Ninth New Collegiate Dictionary,* see "complacency."

not being satisfied with the way things were heading, he jumped into urgent action.

If we want to follow John's example in this area of urgency, we must first become aware of the dangers and deficiencies in our own lives. As you take a moment to look within, do you notice some habits or attitudes forming that are leading you toward a spiritual danger zone? If so, what are they?

_____

_____

Do you see any spiritual deficiencies, areas of neglect or disorder that need attention? If so, what are they?

_____

_____

Once we are aware, we must choose not to be satisfied until we are fulfilling God's top-priority task. What is God telling you to do about these areas?

_____

_____

Now that you've looked inward, focus your thoughts on those around you. Do you know people who may be heading toward a danger zone or faltering in the faith? Who are they?

_____

_____

Pray right now for these individuals. Be sensitive to how God may want to use you to lovingly warn and encourage them. Step out today—their needs are urgent.

 Living Insights STUDY TWO

The second characteristic that we want to look at today is *authenticity*. The Baptizer was like a beautiful diamond on a tray of glass baubles. In stark contrast to the flashy but phony Pharisees, his life sparkled with authenticity. How did his life radiate such quality?

Jewelers know that the value of a gemstone depends on its clarity and cut. The most precious stone is pure; no blemishes mar its capacity to reflect light. Its precise cuts angle and accent the light, firing it and refracting it in a prism of colors.

In the same way, John the Baptizer magnificently reflected and amplified the light of truth without taint or alteration. John was genuine, real, straightforward . . . authentic.

The Pharisees were the opposite. They were two-faced, deceptive, slippery, and suspicious. When the light of truth entered their hearts, one never knew what twists and deformities would occur before it exited their mouths. Rather than reflecting truth in every circumstance, they often exploited it to their own advantage.

What kind of jewel are you? A crafty imitation, or the real McCoy? It all depends on your authenticity. Do people take your word at face value, or do they double-check everything you say? Do you hear yourself saying things you think people want to hear, knowing inside it's not true? Are you kindhearted to some but sour to others?

The Lord searches for authenticity among His people. Read through the following psalm and underline the qualities of authenticity. Notice how these qualities glimmer in the life of John the Baptizer, and seek God's strength so that they may shimmer in your life too.

> O Lord, who may abide in Thy tent?
> Who may dwell on Thy holy hill?
> He who walks with integrity, and works righteousness,
> And speaks truth in his heart.
> He does not slander with his tongue,
> Nor does evil to his neighbor,
> Nor takes up a reproach against his friend;
> In whose eyes a reprobate is despised,
> But who honors those who fear the Lord;
> He swears to his own hurt, and does not change;
> He does not put out his money at interest,
> Nor does he take a bribe against the innocent.
> He who does these things will never be shaken.
> (Ps. 15)

Chapter 8

JOHN,
AS JESUS SAW HIM
Selected Scripture

John's words, like echoes in a canyon, still resound for us today. But also echoing through time are the words spoken by Jesus about John. These words paint a remarkable portrait of John as Jesus saw him. And above all else, they confirm the outstanding character of the austere Baptizer from Judea.

Like a divine character reference, Jesus' words reflect His opinion of John—an opinion without equal. For as the Son of God, He has unparalleled insight into every man's soul, and His judgments bear a matchless integrity. But before we read Christ's endorsement of John, let's take a moment to examine His credentials and discover what sets His opinion and judgments apart from ours.

Regarding Jesus' Opinion and Judgments

The integrity of Christ's opinion rests soundly on four firm foundations: His words are authoritative and inspired, just and objective, righteous and true, and deep and profound. Truly, His opinion is like none other.

Authoritative and Inspired

Jesus' credentials first become clear in John 5, where an intriguing story unfolds. Jesus has healed a man on the Sabbath, which whips up the ire of the Sabbath-conscious Pharisees. They angrily accuse Him of law-breaking and later blasphemy when He justifies His actions by linking them with the Father's (see vv. 1–18). But rather than shying away, Jesus determinedly elaborates on His claim to equality with God.

> Jesus therefore answered and was saying to them, "Truly, truly, I say to you, the Son can do nothing of Himself, unless it is something He sees the Father doing; for whatever the Father does, these things the Son also does in like manner. For the Father loves the Son, and shows Him all things that He

Himself is doing; and greater works than these will He show Him, that you may marvel. For just as the Father raises the dead and gives them life, even so the Son also gives life to whom He wishes. For not even the Father judges anyone, but He has given all judgment to the Son, in order that all may honor the Son, even as they honor the Father. . . . For just as the Father has life in Himself, even so He gave to the Son also to have life in Himself; and He gave Him authority to execute judgment, because He is the Son of Man." (vv. 19–23a, 26–27)

Unlike our judgments, which are backed up only by our own authority and are limited to our own finite, short-sighted perspective, we find that Christ's judgments are authoritative and inspired. They are authoritative because it is the Father who has given Him the right and authority to judge (vv. 22, 27); and they are inspired because Christ shares the same divine nature as the Father.[1]

Just and Objective

Further down in this same chapter we discover the second foundation for the integrity of Jesus' words.

"I can do nothing on My own initiative. As I hear, I judge; and My judgment is just, because I do not seek My own will, but the will of Him who sent Me." (v. 30)

Because Jesus seeks the Father's will instead of His own, His judgment is objective—it doesn't suffer from the selfishness and favoritism that often clouds our opinions. And because of this safeguard of objectivity, His judgments are just—utterly reliable and right.

Righteous and True

The third credential concerning Jesus' opinion is that it is righteous and true. This is revealed in yet another debate with the Jewish leaders, where Jesus responds:

"If a man receives circumcision on the Sabbath that the Law of Moses may not be broken, are you angry

---

1. For example, as the Father gives life, so does the Son (v. 22); as the Father has life in Himself, so also does the Son (v. 26); and as the Father is honored, so also should the Son be honored in the same way (v. 23).

with Me because I made an entire man well on the Sabbath? Do not judge according to appearance, but judge with righteous judgment." (7:23–24)

The implication is that Jesus judges rightly, unlike the religious leaders, who judged according to the way things look—a fact He underscores in chapter 8.

Again therefore Jesus spoke to them, saying, "I am the light of the world; he who follows Me shall not walk in the darkness, but shall have the light of life." The Pharisees therefore said to Him, "You are bearing witness of Yourself; Your witness is not true." Jesus answered and said to them, "Even if I bear witness of Myself, My witness is true; for I know where I came from, and where I am going; but you do not know where I come from, or where I am going. You people judge according to the flesh; I am not judging anyone. But even if I do judge, My judgment is true; for I am not alone in it, but I and He who sent Me." (vv. 12–16)

"You people judge according to the flesh." That's quite an indictment, isn't it? In contrast, Jesus sees what is inside a person, which makes His judgments righteous and true (see also Rev. 16:7; 19:2). Remember what God told the prophet Samuel?

"God sees not as man sees, for man looks at the outward appearance, but the Lord looks at the heart." (1 Sam. 16:7b)[2]

When Jesus judges an individual, it is *never* according to appearance. It is always according to the condition of the heart. He sees motive; we see action. He sees reasons; we see results. We are impressed with looks; He is impressed with character. Likewise, when Jesus saw John, He observed something altogether different than what anyone else saw—He saw his heart.

Deep and Profound

Last, Jesus' opinion comes from His deep and profound knowledge of past, present, and even future events. When His friend

2. For the whole intriguing story surrounding this statement, read 1 Samuel 16:1–13.

Lazarus was gravely ill, Lazarus' sisters sent messengers to Jesus to ask His help (John 11:1–3). But notice Jesus' response:

> "This sickness is not unto death, but for the glory of
> God, that the Son of God may be glorified by it."
> (v. 4b)

Can any of us say that a sickness is "not unto death"? Can any of us confidently tell a man with a terminal illness, "You will not die"? Jesus, however, could see the end result of Lazarus' illness and the purpose behind it as well.

Jesus' knowledge offers immeasurable comfort to the suffering believer. Jesus knows our sorrow. He can see the entire suffering; even death does not escape His view. Remembering that we are safely in His sight reassures us that He cares and that an underlying purpose exists in our pain—God will be glorified.

Now that we've established the impeccable integrity of Jesus' opinion, let's consider His appraisal of John.

Regarding John's Actions and Character

Jesus' thoughts about John can be paraphrased into four nutshell statements. As we examine each one, we'll find that Christ elevates John as a spiritual model to follow.

"John Has Borne Witness to the Truth"

The first commendation is found in John 5.

> "If I alone bear witness of Myself, My testimony is
> not true. There is another who bears witness of Me,
> and I know that the testimony which He bears of
> Me is true. You have sent to John, and *he has borne
> witness to the truth.*" (vv. 31–33, emphasis added)

John trafficked in the realm of truth.[3] This character quality guarded John's reputation; for, as Jesus pointed out, John's truthfulness made him a reliable witness. We, too, are called to live in the

---

3. The word used here for *truth* has a rich heritage in the Greek language. It includes not only provable facts, but also divine reality—that is, the revelation of spiritual matters distinct from myth or fantasy. This supernatural insight should cause us to respond in obedience. *Theological Dictionary of the New Testament*, ed. Gerhard Kittel, trans. and ed. Geoffrey W. Bromiley (Grand Rapids, Mich.: William B. Eerdmans Publishing Co., 1964), vol. 1., pp. 238–39.

liberating realm of truth (8:32), for it is only there that we can experience peace of mind. People with lies littering their past must have good memories to keep each story straight. But people with a truth-filled past are free from anxious fretting and able to enjoy a clean conscience.

"John Was the Burning and Shining Lamp"

Next, Jesus describes John through an astute metaphor.

> "He was the lamp that was burning and was shining and you were willing to rejoice for a while in his light." (John 5:35, emphasis added)

As a lamp, John was not the light, but contained the light. He was merely a vessel out of which the light shone. And as a lamp he had two purposes: the first was to dispel darkness; the second, to guide others. In the same way, God calls us to be containers of light, lamps that shine the truth of Christ to a dark and misguided world.

"John Is More Than a Prophet"

Then, in Matthew's gospel, Jesus commends another facet of John's exemplary character. As is so often the case with Jesus, He starts with simple questions, then builds to a dramatic climax to express a profound point.

> "What did you go out into the wilderness to look at? A reed shaken by the wind? But what did you go out to see? A man dressed in soft clothing? Behold, those who wear soft clothing are in kings' palaces. But why did you go out? To see a prophet? Yes, I say to you, and *one who is more than a prophet.*" (Matt. 11:7b–9, emphasis added)

John, the gritty prophet, was no vacillating, flimsy reed that bent and bowed under every puff of breeze. Neither was he a pampered, petted prince. He was a man shaped by a merciless wilderness, and like the wilderness, his lifestyle was stark and uncompromising. He was a man among men, and a prophet among prophets.

In the same way, we may be required to be more than the average believer, for only God knows what treacherous times lay ahead for us. The kingdom of God has always suffered violent attacks from the enemy, but sadly, God often finds His soldiers soft and complacent. G. K. Chesterton once observed, "The Christian

66

ideal . . . has not been tried and found wanting; it has been found difficult and left untried."[4] What tough times require is an intensity of devotion equal to the intensity of the persecution. God seeks people with drive, purpose, and prophet-like fervor to fight the difficult battles that lay ahead.

"There Has Not Arisen One Greater Than John"

Jesus' sparkling endorsement of John culminates in this final statement.

> "Truly, I say to you, among those born of women *there has not arisen anyone greater than John the Baptist.*" (v. 11a, emphasis added)

Possibly, Jesus was reminiscing about all John's admirable qualities when He made this pronouncement. John's greatness was the sum of his humility, simple devotion, integrity, vision, courage, self-discipline, diligence, and purity.

Regarding You and Me Today

This study concludes the same way it began eight chapters ago, with this "Nobel Prize" Jesus gave John the Baptizer in recognition of his greatness. Can we ever hope to achieve even one facet of such greatness? The key, according to J. Oswald Sanders, is based on the depth of our convictions.

> A small man may entertain strong opinions; a great man cherishes strong convictions. Opinions cost only breath. Convictions may well cost blood. John's convictions were of such an order as to command the attention of the whole nation. To draw a vast crowd, he simply went into the desert and preached repentance, and his convictions deeply affected those who flocked to him.[5]

It comes down to this: Do you *really* believe what you say you believe?

---

4. G. K. Chesterton, as quoted in *Bartlett's Familiar Quotations*, 15th ed., rev. and enl., ed. Emily Morison Beck (Boston, Mass.: Little, Brown and Co., 1980), p. 742.

5. J. Oswald Sanders, *Robust in Faith* (Chicago, Ill.: Moody Press, 1965), p. 181.

For a moment, place yourself beneath the capable and discerning eye of our Savior and consider what kind of character reference He would give you. Use the following questions as your criteria.

- Do I speak the truth and only the truth?

- Is my lamp burning and shining?

- Do the qualities of my character make me rise above the ordinary and the mediocre?

- Am I tough-minded enough to hang in there even when people don't change?

In many ways, the Baptizer was one of a kind, inimitable, and unique. We cannot follow him in every way, for we were not born with angelic fanfare, nor have most of us ever heard God's call to an ascetic desert life. And what are the chances we will die from an executioner's blade?

However, down through the passage of time, coruscating rays of John's life light our skies and beckon us to follow. Against the darkness of our world, John's humility, devotion, conviction, simplicity, zeal, and courage flash as a guiding beacon—a lighthouse of moral integrity. Jesus *was* right, and our sea-worn souls concur: "Among those born of women there has not arisen anyone greater than John the Baptist."

 Living Insights STUDY ONE

God needs more Baptizers—people who are humble yet bold, compassionate yet uncompromising, unshakable yet admitting doubt, fearing no man yet fearing God. He needs people with words which convince, intrigue, and clear a path for Jesus. Voices in the wilderness. Messengers of glory. Are you one of those people? Take some time to evaluate yourself by thoughtfully answering the four questions from the conclusion of our lesson.

1. Have I been speaking the truth lately? If not, why? How can I change?

_____

_____

_____

2. Has my lamp been burning and shining? If not, why? How can I change?

_____

_____

_____

3. Have I been exhibiting qualities that go beyond the ordinary and mediocre? If not, why? How can I change?

_____

_____

_____

4. Have I been tough-minded enough to hang in there even when people don't change? If not, why? How can I change?

_____

_____

_____

Living Insights

Having examined the Baptizer's life from many angles, reflect back on the main themes of his life. The following questions may help you recall key events and principles.

How was John's greatness foreshadowed in the events surrounding his birth? (Chapter 1)

_____

_____

How did his life in the desert prepare him for his ministry? (Chapters 1 and 2)

_____

_____

What was John's message, and how did the different groups receive it? (Chapter 2)

_____

_____

_____

_____

_____

In what ways did John exhibit humility? (Chapter 3)

_____

_____

_____

Why was it important for John to baptize Jesus? (Chapter 4)

_____

_____

Why was John imprisoned, and what was his response to this mistreatment? (Chapter 5)

_____

_____

_____

In what ways does Herod illustrate weakness in comparison to the strength of John? (Chapter 6)

_____

_____

What qualities were the hallmarks of John's character? (Chapters 7 and 8)

_____

_____

_____

What character qualities in John impressed you the most?

_____

_____

_____

_____

_____

_____

_____

_____

_____

BOOKS FOR
PROBING FURTHER

I magine a typical day in the life of John the Baptizer: pray, meditate, find shade from scorching heat, preach, baptize, chase down lunch, pray, meditate, condemn sin, baptize, chase down dinner, find warm cave, sleep.

A typical day in our lives? Shower, pour breakfast from a box, scurry in all directions, make beds, make money, power through lunch, make more money, spend money, microwave dinner, watch TV, fall in bed.

In spite of the differences between our lifestyle and John's, we are undeniably linked to him through his love for Jesus. Normally, we would never cross paths with John; but because of our desire to know his Savior, we humbly come to him and ask to be baptized in that muddy Jordan. There we learn from John lessons on commitment, spiritual discipline, suffering, humility, repentance, and resisting temptation. The following resources are compiled to give you additional insight into these noble character qualities and to inspire you to develop a closer walk with Jesus.

Biography of John the Baptizer

Meyer, F. B. *John the Baptist.* Reprint. Fort Washington, Pa.: Christian Literature Crusade, 1983. Meyer was a world-renowned pastor, author, and speaker in the late nineteenth century, and his tender and penetrating biographies of Bible-characters still speak to us today. You will enjoy the flowing descriptions and analyses this author uses to portray the life of John.

Commitment

White, Jerry. *The Power of Commitment.* Colorado Springs, Colo.: NavPress, 1985. Alarmed by the weak and often failing commit-

---

ments people make today, White focuses on how to make commitments that withstand pressure and time. Covering areas such as your spiritual walk, personal discipline, marriage, children, church, and leadership, he gives solid advice on how to make and keep realistic commitments—ones that give power and integrity to your life.

Humility

Swindoll, Charles R. *Improving Your Serve.* Waco, Tex.: Word Publishing, 1981. Subtitled *The Art of Unselfish Living,* this book details the qualities of a humble, serving person. By examining the definitive servant—Jesus—the author offers helpful insights into the practice of humility.

Repentance

Crabb, Larry. *Inside Out.* Colorado Springs, Colo.: NavPress, 1988. The subject of this book is how to effectively make changes in your life. Not just surface alterations—but deep, personal changes. And the key to doing this, Crabb says, is through true repentance. The author examines this key, focusing especially on its emotional and spiritual implications.

Spiritual Disciplines

Ortlund, Anne. *Disciplines of the Heart.* Waco, Tex.: Word Books, 1987. In short and inspirational chapters, the author paints the inner life of the Christian woman with sensitive brush strokes designed to inspire, prod, and guide.

Piper, John. *Desiring God.* Portland, Oreg.: Multnomah Press, 1986. John the Baptizer may have found true joy in his commitment to Christ, but we often wonder, Can I enjoy Christ too? Piper answers this question with profound insight into several areas of the Christian life: conversion, worship, love, Scripture, prayer, money, marriage, and missions.

Suffering

Carlson, Dwight, and Susan Carlson Wood. *When Life Isn't Fair.* Eugene, Oreg.: Harvest House Publishers, 1989. When Susan Carlson Wood contracted leukemia, she and her father, Dwight, faced the ordeal of their lives. Together they wrestled with the threat of Susan's early death, and together they conquered the insidious illness through the painful procedure of a father-daughter bone marrow transplant. No strangers to suffering, they have written this compassionate book from the heart of their real-life experiences.

Yancey, Philip. *Disappointment with God.* Grand Rapids, Mich.: Zondervan Publishing House, 1988. The Baptizer, despairing in prison, doubted Jesus because nothing was turning out the way he had anticipated. Do you, likewise, ever wonder: Is God fair? Does He really care about me? Why does He allow me to suffer if He loves me? Yancey plows through Scripture and masterfully gleans ripe truths that reveal the God of love and the love He seeks from us in the hard times.

Temptation

Eisenman, Tom L. *Temptations Men Face.* Downers Grove, Ill.: Inter-Varsity Press, 1990. Eisenman writes to men who face the same temptations as Herod Antipas—lust, greed, and power. This frank and thorough book will help you stand against such forces with God's strength.

Mowday, Lois. *The Snare.* Colorado Springs, Colo.: NavPress, 1988. This book, written for women, gives practical advice for avoiding unhealthy entanglements that deceptively promise happiness but more often result in heartache. The author thoughtfully confronts the rationalizations that can blind you to the dangers of immoral emotional and sexual involvement.

ORDERING INFORMATION

Cassette Tapes and Study Guide

This Bible study guide was designed to be used independently or in conjunction with the broadcast of Chuck Swindoll's taped messages on the topic listed below. If you would like to order cassette tapes or further copies of this study guide, please see the information given below and the Order Form provided on the last page of this guide.

JOHN THE BAPTIZER

How do you picture John the Baptizer? Do you see a man clothed in camel hair enjoying a locust-and-honey lunch? Do you see piercing eyes, a coarse beard, and sunburned, leathery skin?

If that is all you see, take another look. This eight-part series on the life of John the Baptizer will open your eyes to a captivating person—a remarkable man who recklessly rebukes the hypocrites but tenderly baptizes repentant sinners, who audaciously scolds powerful Herod but humbly bows before the as-yet-unknown Jesus. From his glorious birth to his ignoble death, this man from the desert will challenge you to a more practical devotion to Christ and a richer understanding of servant-leadership.

Join him at the banks of the Jordan. Listen. Look. Here is a man worth following.

			Calif.*	U.S.	B.C.*	Canada*
JBP	SG	Study Guide	$ 4.26	$ 3.95	$ 5.08	$ 5.08
JBP	CS	Cassette series, includes album cover	25.59	23.75	36.00	34.20
JBP	1–4	Individual cassettes, include messages A and B	5.39	5.00	7.61	7.23

*These prices already include the following charges: for delivery in **California,** 7.75% sales tax; **Canada,** 7% GST and 7% postage and handling (on tapes only); **British Columbia,** 7% GST, 6% British Columbia sales tax (on tapes only), and 7% postage and handling (on tapes only). The prices are subject to change without notice.

JBP	1-A:	*A Most Unusual Baby*—Luke 1:5–25, 57–64, 76–80

JBP   1-A: *A Most Unusual Baby*—Luke 1:5–25, 57–64, 76–80
          B: *Profile of a Strange Evangelist*—Mark 1:1–8

JBP   2-A: *What Are the Secrets of Humility?*—John 1:6–37; 3:22–30
          B: *A River, a Dove, a Voice*—Matthew 3:1–17

JBP   3-A: *When Commitment Leads to Mistreatment*—
              Mark 6:14–20; Matthew 11:1–3
          B: *A Dance of Death*—Mark 6:17–29

JBP   4-A: *He, Being Dead, Still Speaks*—Selected Scripture
          B: *John, as Jesus Saw Him*—Selected Scripture

How to Order by Mail

Simply mark on the order form whether you want the series or individual tapes. Mail the form with your payment to the appropriate address listed below. We will process your order as promptly as we can.

United States: Mail your order to the Sales Department at Insight for Living, Post Office Box 69000, Anaheim, California 92817-0900. If you wish your order to be shipped first-class for faster delivery, add 10 percent of the total order amount. Otherwise, please allow four to six weeks for delivery by fourth-class mail. We accept personal checks, money orders, Visa, or MasterCard in payment for materials. Unfortunately, we are unable to offer invoicing or COD orders.

Canada: Mail your order to Insight for Living Ministries, Post Office Box 2510, Vancouver, British Columbia V6B 3W7. Allow approximately four weeks for delivery. We accept personal checks, money orders, Visa, or MasterCard in payment for materials. Unfortunately, we are unable to offer invoicing or COD orders.

Australia, New Zealand, or Papua New Guinea: Mail your order to Insight for Living, Inc., GPO Box 2823 EE, Melbourne, Victoria 3001, Australia. Please allow six to ten weeks for delivery by surface mail. If you would like your order sent airmail, the delivery time may be reduced. Using the United States price as a base, add postage costs—surface or airmail—to the amount of your order. Please use the chart that follows to determine correct postage. Due to fluctuating currency rates, we can accept only personal checks made payable in U.S. funds, international money orders, Visa, or MasterCard in payment for materials.

Overseas: Other overseas residents should mail their orders to our United States office. Please allow six to ten weeks for delivery by surface mail. If you would like your order sent airmail, the delivery time may be reduced. Using the United States price as a base, add postage costs—surface or airmail—to the amount of your order. Please use the chart that follows to determine correct postage. Due to fluctuating currency rates, we can accept only personal checks made payable in U.S. funds, international money orders, Visa, or MasterCard in payment for materials.

Type of Postage	Postage Cost
Surface	10% of total order
Airmail	25% of total order

For Faster Service, Order by Telephone or FAX

For Visa or MasterCard orders, you are welcome to use one of our toll-free numbers between the hours of 7:00 A.M. and 4:30 P.M., Pacific time, Monday through Friday, or our FAX numbers. The numbers to use from anywhere in the United States are **1-800-772-8888** or FAX (714) 575-5049. To order from Canada, call our Vancouver office using **1-800-663-7639** or FAX (604) 596-2975. Vancouver residents, call (604) 596-2910. Australian residents should phone (03) 872-4606. From overseas, call our Sales Department at (714) 575-5000 in the United States.

Our Guarantee

Our cassettes are guaranteed for ninety days against faulty performance or breakage due to a defect in the tape. For best results, please be sure your tape recorder is in good operating condition and is cleaned regularly.

Note: To cover processing and handling, there is a $10 fee for *any* returned check.

Insight for Living Catalog

Request a free copy of the Insight for Living catalog of books, tapes, and study guides by calling **1-800-772-8888** in the United States or **1-800-663-7639** in Canada.

Order Form

JBP CS represents the entire *John the Baptizer* series in a special album cover, while JBP 1–4 are the individual tapes included in the series. JBP SG represents this study guide, should you desire to order additional copies.

Item	Unit Price Calif.*	U.S.	B.C.*	Canada*	Quantity	Amount
JBP CS	$25.59	$23.75	$36.00	$34.20		$
JBP 1	5.39	5.00	7.61	7.23		
JBP 2	5.39	5.00	7.61	7.23		
JBP 3	5.39	5.00	7.61	7.23		
JBP 4	5.39	5.00	7.61	7.23		
JBP SG	4.26	3.95	5.08	5.08		
					Subtotal	
	Overseas Residents *Pay U.S. price plus 10% surface postage or 25% airmail. Also, see "How to Order by Mail."*					
	U.S. First-Class Shipping *For faster delivery, add 10% for postage and handling.*					
	Gift to Insight for Living *Tax-deductible in the United States and Canada.*					
	Total Amount Due *Please do not send cash.*					$

If there is a balance: ☐ apply it as a donation ☐ please refund
*These prices already include applicable taxes and shipping costs.

Payment by: ☐ Check or money order made payable to Insight for Living or

☐ Credit card (circle one): Visa MasterCard Number _____

Expiration Date _____ Signature _____
We cannot process your credit card purchase without your signature.

Name _____

Address _____

City _____ State/Province _____

Zip/Postal Code _____ Country _____

Telephone (___) _____ Radio Station ___ ___ ___ ___
If questions arise concerning your order, we may need to contact you.

Mail this order form to the Sales Department at one of these addresses:
Insight for Living, Post Office Box 69000, Anaheim, CA 92817-0900
Insight for Living Ministries, Post Office Box 2510, Vancouver, BC, Canada V6B 3W7
Insight for Living, Inc., GPO Box 2823 EE, Melbourne, VIC 3001, Australia

Order Form

JBP CS represents the entire *John the Baptizer* series in a special album cover, while JBP 1–4 are the individual tapes included in the series. JBP SG represents this study guide, should you desire to order additional copies.

Item	Calif.*	Unit Price U.S.	B.C.*	Canada*	Quantity	Amount
JBP CS	$25.59	$23.75	$36.00	$34.20		$
JBP 1	5.39	5.00	7.61	7.23		
JBP 2	5.39	5.00	7.61	7.23		
JBP 3	5.39	5.00	7.61	7.23		
JBP 4	5.39	5.00	7.61	7.23		
JBP SG	4.26	3.95	5.08	5.08		
					Subtotal	
				Overseas Residents *Pay U.S. price plus 10% surface postage or 25% airmail. Also, see "How to Order by Mail."*		
				U.S. First-Class Shipping *For faster delivery, add 10% for postage and handling.*		
				Gift to Insight for Living *Tax-deductible in the United States and Canada.*		
				Total Amount Due *Please do not send cash.*		$

If there is a balance: ☐ apply it as a donation ☐ please refund
*These prices already include applicable taxes and shipping costs.

Payment by: ☐ Check or money order made payable to Insight for Living or

☐ Credit card (circle one): Visa MasterCard Number _____

Expiration Date _____ Signature _____
We cannot process your credit card purchase without your signature.

Name _____

Address _____

City _____ State/Province _____

Zip/Postal Code _____ Country _____

Telephone ( ) _____ Radio Station ___ ___ ___ ___
If questions arise concerning your order, we may need to contact you.

Mail this order form to the Sales Department at one of these addresses:
Insight for Living, Post Office Box 69000, Anaheim, CA 92817-0900
Insight for Living Ministries, Post Office Box 2510, Vancouver, BC, Canada V6B 3W7
Insight for Living, Inc., GPO Box 2823 EE, Melbourne, VIC 3001, Australia

Order Form

JBP CS represents the entire *John the Baptizer* series in a special album cover, while JBP 1–4 are the individual tapes included in the series. JBP SG represents this study guide, should you desire to order additional copies.

Item	Calif.*	Unit Price U.S.	B.C.*	Canada*	Quantity	Amount
JBP CS	$25.59	$23.75	$36.00	$34.20		$
JBP 1	5.39	5.00	7.61	7.23		
JBP 2	5.39	5.00	7.61	7.23		
JBP 3	5.39	5.00	7.61	7.23		
JBP 4	5.39	5.00	7.61	7.23		
JBP SG	4.26	3.95	5.08	5.08		
					Subtotal	
	Overseas Residents *Pay U.S. price plus 10% surface postage or 25% airmail. Also, see "How to Order by Mail."*					
	U.S. First-Class Shipping *For faster delivery, add 10% for postage and handling.*					
	Gift to Insight for Living *Tax-deductible in the United States and Canada.*					
	Total Amount Due *Please do not send cash.*					$

If there is a balance: ☐ apply it as a donation ☐ please refund
*These prices already include applicable taxes and shipping costs.

Payment by: ☐ Check or money order made payable to Insight for Living or

☐ Credit card (circle one): Visa MasterCard Number _____

Expiration Date _____ Signature _____
We cannot process your credit card purchase without your signature.

Name _____

Address _____

City _____ State/Province _____

Zip/Postal Code _____ Country _____

Telephone (___) _____ Radio Station ___ ___ ___ ___
If questions arise concerning your order, we may need to contact you.

Mail this order form to the Sales Department at one of these addresses:
Insight for Living, Post Office Box 69000, Anaheim, CA 92817-0900
Insight for Living Ministries, Post Office Box 2510, Vancouver, BC, Canada V6B 3W7
Insight for Living, Inc., GPO Box 2823 EE, Melbourne, VIC 3001, Australia